NEW DIRECTIONS FOR STUDENT SERVICES

John H. Schuh, *Iowa State University*
EDITOR-IN-CHIEF

Elizabeth J. Whitt, *University of Iowa*
ASSOCIATE EDITOR

Powerful Programming for Student Learning: Approaches That Make a Difference

Debora L. Liddell
University of Iowa

Jon P. Lund
Luther College

EDITORS

Number 90, Summer 2000

JOSSEY-BASS PUBLISHERS
San Francisco

POWERFUL PROGRAMMING FOR STUDENT LEARNING: APPROACHES THAT
MAKE A DIFFERENCE
Debora L. Liddell, Jon P. Lund (eds.)
New Directions for Student Services, no. 90
John H. Schuh, Editor-in-Chief
Elizabeth J. Whitt, Associate Editor

Microfilm copies of issues and articles are available in 16mm and 35mm,
as well as microfiche in 105mm, through University Microfilms Inc., 300
North Zeeb Road, Ann Arbor, Michigan 48106-1346.

ISSN 0164-7970   ISBN 0-7879-5443-8

NEW DIRECTIONS FOR STUDENT SERVICES is part of The Jossey-Bass Higher
and Adult Education Series and is published quarterly by Jossey-Bass, 350
Sansome Street, San Francisco, California 94104-1342. Periodicals postage
paid at San Francisco, California, and at additional mailing offices. Post-
master: Send address changes to New Directions for Student Services,
Jossey-Bass, 350 Sansome Street, San Francisco, California 94104-1342.

New Directions for Student Services is indexed in College Student Personnel Abstracts and Contents Pages in Education.

SUBSCRIPTIONS cost $58.00 for individuals and $104.00 for institutions,
agencies, and libraries. See ordering information page at end of book.

EDITORIAL CORRESPONDENCE should be sent to the Editor-in-Chief,
John H. Schuh, N 243 Lagomarcino Hall, Iowa State University, Ames,
Iowa 50011

Cover photograph by Wernher Krutein/PHOTOVAULT © 1990.

Jossey-Bass Web address: www.josseybass.com

Manufactured in the United States of America on acid-free recycled paper
containing 100 percent recovered waste paper, of which at least 20 percent is postconsumer waste.

Contents

EDITORS' NOTES

Debora L. Liddell, Jon P. Lund

If you want an archival history of what was happening on a particular campus during a particular period, excavate the flyers and posters from any residence hall programming office. These bring to life the issues of the day. Indeed, the student affairs tradition of programming has focused on changing attitudes and behaviors, and facilitating change in students. Certainly, powerful programming was never without an agenda.

In the 1960s there were teach-ins about the Vietnam War, urban violence, and poverty. In fact, we might argue that the entire antiwar movement was, among other powerful things, an incredibly effective cocurricular intervention. In the 1970s, cocurricular programming continued to focus on social justice issues with topics on campus such as birth control, sexism, racism, violence against women, multicultural awareness, environmental advocacy, and nuclear disarmament. Probably one of the most successful programs developed during this period was Earth Day in 1970; its legacy will be long felt. The 1980s found colleges and universities supplementing their academic offerings with programs more congruent to the needs of students in that particular decade. With a recession and high unemployment rates abounding, programming focused on vocational decision making, personal survival skills, and strategies for coping in a rapidly changing world. And with higher education made accessible to students who previously legally were denied those opportunities, we saw the growth of programs on accessibility, disability rights, and success strategies for students with diverse learning styles and needs.

As students continued to come from increasingly diverse backgrounds to our campuses in the 1990s, programming efforts mirrored their diverse needs, focusing on topics such as alcohol awareness, date rape prevention, safe sex, leadership from the margins, community building, roommate conflicts, grief recovery, debt management, single parenthood, sexual harassment, and faith development.

As we think about programming for relevance in this new century, we expect that effective programs will be tied closely to the academic mission of the institution and therefore, by definition, be concerned with outcomes that are learning-oriented. Student affairs educators have a serious obligation to prepare students for lifelong learning. However, because the demands on students' time—as well as our own—keep us from having extended, meaningful informal interactions, we must be very intentional when determining the goals of programming efforts.

Toward that end, Kuh (1999) has written and spoken extensively about the conditions necessary to facilitate student learning: clear goals, measurable outcomes, diverse methodologies and opportunities, intentional reflection, self-knowledge, ability to deal with conflict. Programming, when executed effectively, can be a powerful strategy that incorporates all of these conditions and may indeed come to affect student learning and growth. Powerful programming was never without an agenda. That was true thirty years ago and it remains true today.

This volume, *Powerful Programming for Student Learning: Approaches That Make a Difference,* is designed to assist student affairs professionals as they reflect on, plan for, implement, and evaluate programming interventions on college and university campuses. Programming has been and will continue to be a viable vehicle for transmitting knowledge, affecting skills development, changing attitudes, and helping students become successful, both on and off campus. Accordingly, there is a need for knowledgeable and ethical programmers on college and university campuses, individuals who are adept at tailoring and evaluating programming interventions so that they may positively contribute to increasing students' learning and growth.

This volume is intended for student affairs professionals in general and program planners in particular. We believe it will also appeal to other individuals not associated with student affairs units who have, either in whole or in part, functional responsibility for conducting meaningful, learning-centered programming targeted toward college students. Graduate educators may consider adopting it as a textbook for aspiring professionals.

In Chapter One, Diane Cooper and Sue Saunders discuss the importance of assessing individual and group needs, as well as environmental issues such as culture, norms, and politics, as the building blocks upon which successful programming is built. They provide insights into various theoretical models of programming and suggest several skills and competencies necessary for effective program assessment.

Debora Liddell, Steve Hubbard, and Rochelle Werner, in Chapter Two, highlight the importance of establishing specific goals and objectives prior to undertaking programming initiatives. The authors also discuss various program delivery methods and tie programming to learning by exploring the use of reflection and reflection activities as one component of good programming.

In Chapter Three, Ann Highum and Jon Lund examine the nature of programming partnerships and the ways in which these partnerships hold promise for increasing student learning. The authors describe several types of programming partnerships and then illustrate these partnerships using four brief case studies from colleges and universities of varying institutional types. They conclude the chapter by reflecting on a few of the most significant partnership aspects that led to programming success.

Chapter Four provides the reader with concrete nuts and bolts suggestions for successful programming. The author, Celine Hartwig, provides suggestions for managing programming aspects from formulating the task timeline to publicizing the program. She concludes her chapter with a thorough program implementation checklist to assist planners in all details related to program planning and delivery.

Margaret Healy, in Chapter Five, explores the important and often overlooked final step of programming, determining whether or not the programming intervention has helped students learn, grow, or change in the intended ways. Healy describes the process of program evaluation, including identifying the intended growth dimensions (that is, knowledge, skills, or attitudes) and considerations in the actual design of the evaluation. She concludes by exploring topics such as collecting data, selecting instruments, and reporting results.

In the ensuing two chapters, we have selected two prevalent programming topics—multicultural competence and sexual violence—to represent specific programming issues of considerable currency on college and university campuses today. Mary Howard-Hamilton, in Chapter Six, highlights good practices in the delivery of diversity programming. In Chapter Seven, Tracy Davis explores the equally important and timely topic of rape prevention programs, specifically those targeted toward men.

Finally, Heather O'Neill, in Chapter Eight, provides an overview of a number of specific promising programs already in place on a number of college and university campuses. Specifically, her chapter illuminates interesting service learning, leadership, community-building, alcohol awareness, and diversity programs on almost thirty college campuses.

This editorial partnership, like many collaborations in programming, began as a sort of professional blind date. We were introduced by a mutual acquaintance for the purpose of putting this volume together. Debora's experiences as a faculty member at a research institution and Jon's background in student affairs at a private college complemented one another well. It was our objective to present a useful model for program planning, implementation, and evaluation that focuses on student learning and is appropriate for a variety of campuses and students. We hope we have succeeded in our goal to present powerful programming as learning-focused and accessible on your campus.

Debora L. Liddell
Jon P. Lund
Editors

Reference

Kuh, G. D. "Partnerships for Learning." Paper presented at The University of Iowa College of Education, Iowa City, April 16, 1999.

DEBORA L. LIDDELL is associate professor in the Division of Counseling, Rehabilitation, and Student Development at The University of Iowa in Iowa City. She teaches in the Student Development in Postsecondary Education Program and has prior experience working in residence life, women's centers, and minority and international student programs.

JON P. LUND is assistant dean for student life at Luther College in Decorah, Iowa. He serves as director of both career development and college assessment at the institution.

1

*Prior to designing and implementing any programmatic
initiative, the programmer must consider the assessment
of individual and group needs as well as environmental or
cultural dimensions.*

Assessing Programmatic Needs

Diane L. Cooper, Sue A. Saunders

Andreas (1993) points out that no matter in which student affairs area we
are employed, chances are very good that we will be called upon to work on
some phase of programming, from assessment and design through implementation and evaluation. Often, we arrive at a new institution eager to
begin our position and are immediately faced with a set of program initiatives that seem outdated, unnecessary, underused, or redundant. When we
try to ascertain why programs are in place, we are met with responses such
as "we have always done it that way," or "because Dr. X thought it would be
a good idea," or "because we had a problem with that once," or "the *Chron-
icle* says it is a problem nationally, so we assumed it is a problem here."
These difficulties and responses, as well as the fact that student affairs posi-
tions require some involvement in programming, all point to a need to
know how to conduct assessment prior to both initiating new programs and
refining or redesigning programs currently in place. This chapter identifies
the models of program planning and discusses the differences between environmental assessment and needs assessment.

The term *program* may be used to describe a functional unit such as
international student programs, a series of activities such as leadership
development programs, or a one-shot event such as a résumé writing workshop (Barr, Keating, and Associates, 1985). Each of these types of programs
requires a somewhat different assessment approach, which may also need
to take place on several levels:

Individual or group level—assessing the skills, knowledge, attitudes, and
beliefs of individuals who will attend or take part in the programming initiative

Environment level—assessing the culture, norms, politics, stakeholders, and organizational structure for issues and methodologies to address as well as those to leave alone

Considering both individual needs and environmental presses will greatly increase the likelihood of a successful programming endeavor. Data collected prior to designing a program initiative, even prior to the planning process, will help define what students or other target audiences need, what program components should be included, when the program should occur, and how and by whom it should be delivered (Hanson and Yancy, 1985).

Assessment has come to mean a variety of things in higher education. Astin, in *Assessment for Excellence* (1991), stated that assessment includes "the gathering of information of students, staff . . . information may or may not be in numerical form, but the basic motive for gathering it is to improve the functioning of the institution and its people" (p. 2). Upcraft and Schuh (1996) define assessment as "any effort to gather, analyze, and interpret evidence which describes institutional, departmental, divisional, or agency effectiveness" (p. 18). Finally, Erwin (1996) notes that assessment is a "process for defining, measuring, collecting, analyzing, and using information to enrich the educational experience of students" (p. 416). All of these definitions consider the importance of (1) collecting data, (2) making meaning out of the data, and (3) using the data to bring about change. Assessment for program design should take into account those three basic steps.

Models of Program Planning

Even though several program planning models exist, most of them do not describe specific assessment strategies as a starting point. All of these models, however, do provide a theoretical basis for program development, implementation, and evaluation. Each of these models will be briefly discussed in terms of how each addresses the assessment process.

The CUBE. Morrill, Oetting, and Hurst (1974) introduced a programming model that was based on a classification system in counseling outreach programs. The *CUBE* is a three-dimensional model that includes (1) the target of an intervention or program, (2) the purpose of the intervention or program, and (3) the method of delivery for the intervention or program. Using this model, a programmer can consider who should receive the benefits of the program—individual, primary group, associational group, or institution—and define the goal of the intervention as being either preventative, remedial, or developmental. Finally, the methods that will be used to deliver the program (direct, training and consultation, or media) can be designed. This model seems to assume that a preassessment is conducted or at least discussed by those using the model. Yet this particular model does not prescribe the actual process that practitioners should use.

Moore and Delworth. The Western Interstate Commission on Higher Education (WICHE) sanctioned the program development model organized by Moore and Delworth (1976). The focus of this model is on the program planning team and the various activities it develops. However, assessment is not listed as an early task. The assessment process is assumed within the expertise of those invited to be part of the planning team and the discussions that take place to generate the program idea. Once they agree upon the program idea, they recommend a resource and institutional assessment to decide whether or not the idea is needed in the current environment.

Barr and Keating. This model is based on both the CUBE and WICHE models. Barr and Keating acknowledged that assessment was necessary for this model to be implemented successfully. Hanson and Yancy's chapter in Barr, Keating, and Associates (1985) discusses in detail the process of gathering data necessary to determine the program needs for institutions.

Barr and Cuyjet. More recently, Barr and Cuyjet (1991) proposed a six-step program planning process that begins with assessment as the first step. They outline five assessment areas to be considered by program planners: (1) current operation, (2) student characteristics, (3) needs, (4) institutional environments, and (5) resource environment. The current operation assessment is a consideration of those activities and programs that are currently in place within the institution. Often, much time and money can be saved through a thorough review of programs currently offered across the campus. Sometimes, those programs may need only better advertising or an augmentation of material to meet the needs of a different population.

Next, Barr and Cuyjet recommend a review of the current student population with respect to their characteristics and needs. Who are the students attending your institution? What skill deficiencies exist? Where do the students live and congregate on campus that might be a good programming site? In this step, attend to the needs of students of color as well as students in other identifiable groups on campus.

Cuyjet. Cuyjet (1996) adds another element to the assessment process in his most recent discussion of program development. He cautions student affairs practitioners to consider past programming efforts, to look at "what has been tried before, and determine why past programs succeeded or failed" (p. 404). In some cases this is more easily said than done. As mentioned earlier, one often starts a new job with little evaluative data from past endeavors. In that case, anecdotal data may be all that is available.

Although other programming models exist, the ones listed earlier are most commonly referred to in the literature. What emerges from a study of these models is the need for student affairs practitioners to develop skills related to assessment and evaluation in order to be good program developers. It is impossible to develop good, ongoing programs without preassessing needs as well as designing appropriate post-program evaluations.

Program Assessment Skills Needed by Student Affairs Administrators

Effective program assessment requires a number of skills and abilities. Even though most of these skills should be cultivated during graduate training, one must keep up with new assessment principles and technologies in order to stay current. Furthermore, as the designers of assessments decide what questions to ask, whom to ask, and what programs or services would be useful to assess, they must continually monitor their attitudes, assumptions, and perceptions to be confident of their validity. What follows is a brief list of skills and attitudes that practitioners should have.

Understand the Methodology of Assessment. Understanding assessment methodology is no easy task. Multiple and conflicting definitions exist, even of assessment itself. Furthermore, learning the techniques required for even rudimentary qualitative and quantitative assessments requires several graduate courses; teaching these techniques is clearly beyond the scope of this chapter. A few basic concepts deserve mention, however. If practitioners wish to go beyond simple measures of student satisfaction with programs, they must use a standard definition of assessment (such as the one included in the beginning of this chapter). Using a standard definition and communicating it to colleagues, respondents, supervisors, and recipients of assessment reports prevents the unnecessary debates about whether a particular activity is assessment, research, or evaluation. Using a standard accepted definition also gives credibility to the project. The discussion of terminology contained in *Assessment in Student Affairs: A Guide for Practitioners* (Upcraft and Schuh, 1996) provides a comprehensive framework to communicate assessment concepts in a fashion understandable to a variety of audiences.

The irony of the student affairs profession is that, often, those asked to be in charge of program assessment are the midlevel professionals who have not taken a research or measurement course in several years. Some colleges and universities are lucky enough to have within the division of student affairs an assessment specialist who is available to assist with design and implementation of studies. At many institutions, however, there are no staff members who have expertise in student affairs theory, practice, and measurement and design. Fortunately, most campuses have social science faculty members, an institutional research staff, or an academic assessment office staff who have expertise in designing and conducting studies. In addition, workshops about the techniques involved in student affairs assessment are typically offered at the ACPA and NASPA national conventions and at many regional or state student affairs conferences. The American Association for Higher Education offers an assessment forum each June that is designed for academic and student affairs professionals to share exemplary programs and to discuss techniques.

Understand the Institutional Priorities and Values. Before even beginning to assess a program, a wise practitioner will ask why the assessment is necessary (Upcraft and Schuh, 1996). The purpose of most program assessments is to ensure that organizational mission and goals are addressed. The organizational goals relevant to a particular program might be to promote student learning and personal development, to use scarce resources efficiently, or to respond to a particular campus crisis or dilemma.

The values of an organization also affect the purpose and structure of assessment. Upcraft and Schuh state that "values drive not only *what* we choose to assess, but also *how* we choose to do so. When questions about the organizational mission and values are skipped over, assessment threatens to be an exercise in measuring what's easy rather than what is needed" (1996, p. 22). For example, determining whether an expensive, time-intensive program to improve the academic success of members of Greek letter organizations justifies its cost requires an understanding of institutional priorities and values. Does the university see itself as having special responsibility for this segment of the student population? Will attention to this group result in a reduction of time and resources available for other segments? Will improvement in academic performance of members of Greek letter organizations assist in achieving the institution's goal of improved retention?

Understanding the institutional priorities and values requires the ability to gain access to both the explicit and implicit priorities and values. Typically, one can read the explicit priorities and values in the institution or organization's mission statement or its strategic plan. Understanding the implicit priorities and values requires more skill and is more susceptible to bias due to limited information or individual preferences. For example, a housing professional who wants to assess the effectiveness of residence hall social programs might be unaware of the chief student affairs officer's and president's priority to emphasize educational interventions. So even if the social programs are assessed to be highly appealing to students and are shown to contribute to students' willingness to stay in residence halls, social program resources might ultimately be reduced in the interest of promoting more educational efforts.

Understand Organizational and Group Dynamics. Those who complete effective program assessment must have the ability to understand the dynamics of the organizations and groups within which they work. Dynamics involve the patterns or norms of organizational decision making. For example, on some campuses individuals external to residence halls, such as academic advisors, campus police, or even the college president, are very interested in assessment of programs designed to prevent substance abuse or sexual assault. Therefore, at these institutions it would be wise for multiple stakeholders to be involved in the planning process.

The *halo effect* is another group dynamics concept in which, for example, students enrolled in a résumé writing workshop facilitated by an attractive and popular career development program facilitator may be more likely to judge the handouts to be very well written, even though a staff member reviewing the handouts sees typographical errors and problems with layout.

To counteract the halo effect it is helpful to obtain assessments other than simple self-reports (Nisbett and Wilson, 1978). Assessing students' knowledge in addition to their perceptions or having professional peers review workshop materials are ways to eliminate the halo effect.

Another concept from the literature of group dynamics is the *Hawthorne effect* (Mayo, 1945). Essentially, researchers have demonstrated that when individuals are aware that someone interested in their opinion is assessing them, their behavior changes from what might be otherwise expected. If, for example, students know that their responses to an opinion questionnaire about a particular program affect the continuation of that program, their responses might be either more positive or more negative than if they were sharing opinions with peers who had no influence on program decisions. Again, the wise assessor will view assessment results cautiously, recognizing that the process of assessment itself can affect results.

Understand Assessor's Assumptions. If an assessor wanted to complete an assessment to determine if women students perceive a need for programs on peer sexual harassment, it might be tempting to query only women students. This approach is flawed because the assessor is assuming that only women are affected by sexual harassment—when, in fact, sexual harassment may be affecting students across gender boundaries. Men can be harassed and also are affected by a campus climate that does not openly address harassment.

The assumptions an assessor makes affects the design, implementation, analysis, and reporting of results. All elements of assessment are vulnerable to unintended bias. Assessors may analyze data without attention to interaction effects. So single categories, such as race, age, gender, or residential status, would be analyzed as individual grouping variables that may mask the real possibility that African American women commuter students may be more like other commuter students than those in their ethnic or gender groups.

How then might one ascertain whether unexamined assumptions affect assessment decisions? One way to determine whether written surveys or interview questions are asking what is intended is to conduct a simple pilot test of the measurement device or strategy. To find out if an analysis of conclusions from interviews is correct, an assessor could do a member check, giving participants the opportunity to refute or add to the assessor's interpretations.

As mentioned earlier, assessment as a precursor to program design needs to take place on both a macro- (environmental) and a micro- (individuals and groups) level on campus. We will now explore implications for both types of assessment.

Assessing the Environment

The institutional environment deserves specific attention in the assessment process. It is critical to assess both the formal environment as well as the informal structure to get an accurate picture of the campus. The data may come from a variety of sources and be collected in both qualitative as well as quantitative forms. Some data can be obtained in an unobtrusive manner from university records and databases. The increased use of technology on campus has also helped with this data collection. Student identification cards are now used as admission to various student services units, so tracking use patterns can be part of normal operations. In addition, data collected from students during the admissions and orientation process is very useful for program planning. More sophisticated programs involve longitudinal tracking of student progress with pre- and posttesting times as a requirement on some campuses for collecting outcomes data. No matter whether a campus has a sophisticated model or practitioners rely on interviews with students during lunch at the dining hall, understanding who students are and what they need to be successful in college should help dictate programmatic initiatives.

Upcraft and Schuh noted that "environmental assessment determines and evaluates how various elements and conditions of the college campus milieu affect student learning and growth" (1996, p. 167). Knowing this type of information will help the student affairs programmer design a program initiative that accurately reflects and fits into the current environment. However, as Barr and Cuyjet pointed out, "assessment of the institutional environment can be a more difficult task than that of assessing student needs" (1991, p. 716). Successful programs take place in an environment that is supportive of the initiative, is characterized by a healthy political climate, and includes the voices of the various constituencies who may have vested interests in the programs and their outcomes. Finally, one cannot complete this phase of the program planning process without assessing the resources, staff, money, and physical environment available for the programming initiative. A deficiency in any one of the three areas could make the difference between a successful program and a waste of valuable staff time invested in the planning process.

Environmental Areas to Consider

Strange (1991) outlined four areas of the campus environment as physical, human aggregate, structural organizational, and perceptual (part of which is the political). Each of these warrants further discussion as we consider how to appropriately assess the environment in which the program initiative will take place.

Physical Environment. This part of the college campus environment contains all the physical aspects including "natural and synthetic that influence human behavior within them" (Strange, 1991, p. 162). But also the "physical features of the environment influence the extent to which individuals are attracted to and satisfied within any given setting" (p. 165). In some ways this aspect of the environment also constrains some of the student programs that can take place. For example, if a campus does not have, or have access to, a ropes course, this type of group programming experience could not take place.

How may one assess the physical environment? Observation is an important first step. Much can be deduced about student behavior and any corresponding needs just by watching how students interact within a particular physical environment. For example, do students seem segregated by physical constraints or are they moving about and together comfortably? Are more students trying to get into the Career Services Center than that space can readily accommodate? If so, programming may need to occur in different physical locations around campus.

In addition to observing how space is used, programmers need to assess the quality of the programming space available. It may be difficult to provide programming on certain topics or to teach specific skills in an environment devoid of specific accoutrements.

Human Aggregate Environment. All inhabitants of the campus physical environment and their unique characteristics make up the total human aggregate. The people along with their patterns of involvement, interactions, behaviors, knowledge, and skills taken together can be a powerful force on campus. Assessing this aspect of the environment can be very complicated. Some inexpensive methods include observation as well as interviewing. In addition, some assessment instruments could be used to ascertain the usage patterns and behaviors of students, thus providing useful information for program planners. For example, the *College Student Experiences Questionnaire* (Pace and Kuh, 1998) provides assessment data regarding the usage patterns of various student services, organizations, involvement with faculty, as well as a variety of other curricular and cocurricular behaviors. Armed with this knowledge, practitioners are able to design programs based on the needs of the students in that particular environment.

Structural Organizational Environment. The mission, goals, and objectives of an institution, as well as the manner in which the people in it are organized, compose the structural organizational environment. Ideally, the manner in which the institution is organized reflects the stated mission, goals, and objectives. That is not, however, always the case. Assessing this aspect involves reviewing reporting lines, level of hierarchy, mission, purposes, budgets, and roles in the structure.

Perceptual Environment. The perceptions that an individual has about an environment are based on the subjective viewpoint from which he or she interacts with the environment. Assessing these perceptions can, and perhaps should (Erwin, 1996), be accomplished in both qualitative and quantitative methods. Interviews, focus groups, and a review of user evaluations can all be effective methods for assessing the perceptions of individuals living and working in the environment. A number of instruments are also on the market to assist practitioners in collecting quantitative data from students about the quality of campus life, effectiveness of student services, and satisfaction with the student experience.

The Political Environment. The political environment also needs to be mentioned here because even the best-designed program can fail if the program designer does not take into account aspects of the political process in assessing the need for a program. Recipes for failure might include conducting a program on a socially controversial topic on which the institution's president has taken a firm stand in the media or conducting alcohol education programs on a football Saturday. More often than not, the politics are much more subtle and difficult to ascertain. Brown and Podolske (1993), in their work discussing political models of program evaluation, note that skills needed to assess this aspect of the environment range from "being a good observer, thinker, and politician to possessing high-level consultation, negotiation, research design, and measurement abilities" (p. 217). We would argue that the same skills required in order to be a good evaluator are also required in order to be good at assessing the environment in which the programming will take place.

Collecting Environmental Assessment Data

Environmental assessment data may be collected in a number of ways. For example, if I am a new area coordinator for a residence life operation, I may be very interested in examining the current needs, behaviors, skills, and knowledge of the students living in the halls. I decide that I will gather data to make my decision from several sources including

Conducting focus groups in each hall by inviting a random group of eight to twelve students to dinner, where I can ask them questions about their living environment (Jacobi, 1991)

Administering the University Residence Environmental Scales to a stratified, random sample based on class standing, race, and gender

Visiting students via floor meetings throughout the semester to ask about the quality of the living environment

Reviewing disciplinary records and discussing the living environment with students who take part in the hall judicial process

Reviewing incident reports to assess the level and types of physical damage occurring in each hall

Using part of several Resident Assistant staff meetings and hall council meetings to discuss perceptions of the quality of residence hall life

These various assessment processes will provide the area coordinator with a wealth of information about the residence hall environment, the residents living there, and their behaviors. In this example, the area coordinator may use the assessment data in a variety of ways to select and design appropriate program initiatives.

Assessing Student Needs

Done properly, assessments of student needs can provide valuable direction for programming efforts. Several principles can make needs assessment results a valid tool for developing programs that will lead to student learning and personal development.

Needs Are Different from Wants. This principle seems obvious, but the concept becomes complicated in practice. Needs, according to Upcraft and Schuh (1996), are those factors, conditions, services, and resources which are necessary for a student to achieve educational goals and objectives. For example, a Dean's Student Advisory Committee tells the dean that to have a meaningful program series on ethnic diversity, the campus needs a kick-off speaker who is well recognized and respected by students, like a congressman or a television news commentator known for powerful insights on the benefits of multicultural communities. Even if the majority of students were to report this "need," the celebrity status of the speaker might not facilitate achievement of the program's educational goals to develop appreciation of ethnic diversity. The celebrity speaker may draw students, but may not be informed enough to send a message that is meaningful and pertinent to the local situation. It is not always clear that a well-known speaker will contribute to students' achievement of the university's goals to value diverse persons and perspectives. The students' perceived need for a big-name speaker is likely to be a want or a desire.

In certain situations, however, a high-status celebrity speaker could meet an institutional or community need. If a celebrity could bring in additional positive publicity about the university's commitment to diversity, perhaps more minority students would apply, thereby meeting an important institutional need.

It is important to recognize that often what is portrayed as meeting a student need is instead addressing either an institutional, community, or administrative need, or a fervent desire on the part of a considerable segment of the student body. In practice, students' desires may often provide good justification for programming decisions, such as purchase of a karaoke machine or providing less-than-nutritious food at residence hall functions. It is important to recognize, however, that these programming decisions are, at best, tenuously related to student needs.

Include Multiple Populations. All too often when student needs are assessed, only students themselves are queried. Secondhand sources of information about students' educational needs, such as faculty or staff, can provide valuable perspectives on students. Faculty and/or staff who have close connections with students and who are veterans at the institution are often excellent participants in qualitative or informal assessments of student needs. Because of their knowledge of the institution and experience working with multiple generations of students, these individuals can be very perceptive and insightful about the student experience.

Often, those most likely to participate in the informal assessments so important for determining students' needs are those with whom administrators have the most contact—the student leaders. Surveying students in hopes of getting input from nonleaders often results in such low response rates that results simply are not useful. Researchers have designed many creative inducements such as prizes, food, and gift certificates to increase students' response to surveys. These incentives do improve response rates somewhat but the cost can, over time, be prohibitive. Other ways to encourage nonleaders to respond to needs assessments include

- Asking faculty to allow their students to be surveyed during class time
- Having students or employees hand a survey to individuals when they are waiting in line for event tickets
- Using focus groups scheduled at convenient times and places
- Scheduling time for informal conversations with students in the dining facilities

Consider Using a Theoretical Basis for Assessing Needs. Evans's (1985) study of needs assessment processes found that items on theory-based questionnaires were judged to be more relevant to students than those on empirically based surveys. Student development theory provides excellent guidance to help assessors determine student needs and measure outcomes of interventions. A variety of developmental theories, including those appropriate for underrepresented populations, provide excellent foundations for high-quality assessment. The recent book entitled *Student Development in College: Theory, Practice, and Research* (Evans, Forney, and Guido-DiBrito, 1998), provides excellent summaries of developmental theories along with explanations of the related assessment tools. In addition, the authors outline validity and reliability data for each of the instruments they discuss.

Designed to assess psychosocial development of college students, the Student Developmental Task and Lifestyle Assessment (Winston, Miller, and Cooper, 1999) is frequently used. Because this instrument can be used to compare group scores at one institution with national norms, it can be used to assess both students' psychosocial needs as well as growth following an intervention.

Using standardized instruments, however, is not the only way to create assessments based on theory. Student development theory is useful in determining what qualitative questions the assessor should construct. Furthermore, theory assists assessors in data analysis and interpretation. For example, let us suppose that the results from focus groups indicated that college freshmen felt that the most effective eating disorder–prevention programs were those that featured a survivor of an eating disorder who could tell students the importance of recognizing symptoms early. One could interpret that many of these students were in Perry's (1968) basic duality (Position 1), by which students typically believe that a meaningful educational experience must have an expert to deliver the correct answers.

Developmental theories also have implications for the details of program planning. For example, if a group of student affairs professionals wanted to design a program to promote responsible use of alcohol, they might interview students, constructing their questions based on Chickering and Reisser's (1993) psychosocial developmental theory. This theory posits that students early in their college careers are focused on autonomy and expressing independence, but are later more likely to understand that their actions affect the whole community. Let us suppose that the results of the interviews of freshmen indicated that many students felt that programs about alcohol use were a waste of time, especially if conducted by a faculty or staff member who had disciplinary responsibilities. Upperclassmen, on the other hand, felt that there was some benefit in these programs to help classmates who might have problems with alcohol abuse. The program planners might, therefore, make certain that some substance abuse–prevention programs were conducted by facilitators other than the familiar faculty and staff. Programs might also include comfortable group discussions between upperclassmen and freshman students in an environment that was safe and secure for students who had personal or family problems with alcohol.

Use Methods Appropriate to the Problem. In their discussion of myths and facts about assessment, Schuh and Upcraft (1998) suggest flexibility when determining methodology. Neither qualitative nor quantitative methods are superior in every case. The context and nature of the problem dictate the method. In many cases, because of the complexity of issues such as student learning, retention, the creation of environments that promote healthy lifestyles, or students' psychosocial development, no one method can capture the essence of a situation.

It is often tempting for student affairs to simply administer surveys to students to determine what they want in terms of educational programs about complex issues. Such an approach might be highly appropriate if the decision were about which concerts to book or to determine whether additional writing workshops were warranted.

But with emotionally and politically charged issues such as ethnic diversity or sexuality education, it is wise to avoid the broad-based survey approach because it is nearly impossible to understand the motivation and complex feelings behind the answers. If surveyed, students on a particular campus might conceivably report that there is no need for more programs on relationships between diverse ethnic groups. Some students may draw that conclusion because they assume the divisiveness at their college is so severe that no program alone will alleviate the problem. Others might answer that there is no need because they see few problems among ethnic groups at their institution. Others might be expressing antipathy toward what they perceive to be the institution's political correctness. Still others might feel that they had already covered issues of ethnic diversity in high school.

Functional Unit-Level Program Assessment

Table 1.1 illustrates how one student affairs functional unit, career services, might consider the skills, knowledge, behaviors, and beliefs that that office believes it should address through programming for students. The unit in question needs to ask one important question: What do we do to help our clients (students) change, develop, acquire skills, or learn by virtue of their interaction with our programs? All program staff must periodically ask this question and evaluate how the current offerings are addressing the needs of the clientele. The answer to this question should also guide program development and be used as part of the general program review.

Communicating and Using Results

Upcraft and Schuh (1996) note that even if you have done everything right in the program assessment process, the results can be ignored if they are not reported appropriately to the decision makers and stakeholders. They go on to point out that "the most common mistake investigators make is to send a complete and comprehensive report [modeled after a dissertation] to all intended audiences" (p. 281). As busy professionals who receive many reports, flyers, and other written material, college and university administrators may miss important assessment findings if the reporting is not done in an appropriate manner.

Citing Suskie's (1992) work on survey research, Upcraft and Schuh (1996) point out that it is critical to first determine who needs to receive a report of assessment results. Second, a decision should be made regarding the format to be used for reporting the results. Does a particular audience only need a page or two summarizing the findings or will this stakeholder require a formal complete report including tables and statistical analyses?

Table 1.1. Career Services

	In What Ways Do We Want to Help Students Grow and Change by Virtue of Interacting with Our Office?	What Programs or Services Do We Offer (or Need to Provide) to Facilitate This Growth and Development?
Skills	Constructing a résumé	Program—How to design an effective résumé
Behaviors	How to interact with prospective employers	Service—Mock interviewing with staff
Knowledge	Exploring job opportunities	Service—WWW access in office
Beliefs	Dress for success	Program—How to prepare for your first job

In preparing the report it is critical to keep the writing as readable as possible for all intended audiences.

A note of caution should be given here. Upcraft and Schuh (1996) would advise that care be given to the reporting of particularly negative, sensitive, or controversial findings from assessment. "Probably the most difficult situation for an investigator comes when he or she realizes that the results of a study will not please the decision makers who commissioned it. Worse yet is the situation in which the results show that the decision makers appear to be part of the problem" (p 284). Assessment conducted to assess the needs of individuals, groups, or of the environment can, in fact, produce troubling results. It is politically prudent for assessors to encourage decision makers to be prepared for all possible outcomes of an assessment.

How and to whom the information is to be reported is often a difficult decision. Of course, it would be unethical to withhold the information or to share the results in misleading ways, so the information must be relayed. Perhaps including the decision makers along the way in the report writing will help move the process along and ensure that no one is surprised by the final report.

Final Thoughts

Assessment is a complex, intricate, precise, and detailed process that uses measurement to gauge student needs and outcomes. At the same time, however, those who conduct assessments must keep their eyes on the bigger picture of institutional trends, environmental impacts, and the political implications of potential and actual findings. Because of increased attention to accountability and efficient use of valuable resources, facility with program assessment is fast becoming an expectation for all levels of staff. No longer is simple anecdotal information sufficient to keep programs or major initiatives healthy and protected from budget cuts.

All too often, an individual's skills in assessment become rusty shortly after the completion of graduate training. Professionals would be well served to practice assessment skills both to determine individual student needs and to ascertain what characteristics in the institutional environment have the potential to influence programming efforts. If professionals are continuously assessing the need for programs, determining environmental constraints and supports, and evaluating programming outcomes, not only will they improve their assessment competence but they will also gain credibility within institutional environments that increasingly embrace precise measurement of effectiveness.

Like any powerful tool, assessment requires careful use. Practitioners must make sure that they know their data collection methodologies, are skilled in analysis of information, are unbiased in interpretation of findings, and sensitive to possible implications of their reports. A poorly constructed assessment, unsupported interpretations, or poorly drafted reports are worse, in most cases, than no assessment at all. Good assessment takes both time and institutional commitment and may affect the amount of attention devoted to other day-to-day operations (Schuh and Upcraft, 1998). Yet if student affairs programs are to compete for scarce institutional resources, assessment and evaluation must take priority.

References

Andreas, R. E. "Program Planning." In M. J. Barr (ed.), *The Handbook of Student Affairs Administration*. San Francisco: Jossey-Bass, 1993.

Astin, A. W. *Assessment for Excellence*. Phoenix, Ariz.: Oryx Press, 1991.

Barr, M. J., and Cuyjet, M. J. "Program Development and Implementation." In T. K. Miller, R. B. Winston, Jr., and Associates (eds.), *Administration and Leadership in Student Affairs*. (2nd ed.) Muncie, Ind.: Accelerated Development, 1991.

Barr, M. J., Keating, L. A., and Associates (eds.). *Developing Effective Student Services Programs: Systematic Approaches for Practitioners*. San Francisco: Jossey-Bass, 1985.

Brown, R. D., and Podolske, D. L. "A Political Model for Program Evaluation." In M. J. Barr (ed.), *The Handbook of Student Affairs Administration*. San Francisco: Jossey-Bass, 1993.

Chickering, A. W., and Reisser, L. R. *Education and Identity*. (2nd ed.) San Francisco: Jossey-Bass, 1993.

Cuyjet, M. J. "Program Development and Group Advising." In S. R. Komives and D. B. Woodard (eds.), *Student Services: A Handbook for the Profession*. (3rd ed.) San Francisco: Jossey-Bass, 1996.

Erwin, T. D. "Assessment, Evaluation, and Research." In S. R. Komives and D. B. Woodard (eds.), *Student Services: A Handbook for the Profession*. (3rd ed.) San Francisco: Jossey-Bass, 1996.

Evans, N. J. "Needs Assessment Methodology: A Comparison of Results." *Journal of College Student Development,* 1985, *26,* 107–114.

Evans, N. J., Forney, D. S., and Guido-DiBrito, F. *Student Development in College: Theory, Research, and Practice*. San Francisco: Jossey-Bass, 1998.

Hanson, G. R., and Yancy, B. D. "Gathering Information to Determine Program Needs." In M. J. Barr, L. A. Keating, and Associates (eds.), *Developing Effective Student Services Programs: Systematic Approaches for Practitioners*. San Francisco: Jossey-Bass, 1985.

Jacobi, M. "Focus Group Research: A Tool for the Student Affairs Professional." *NASPA Journal,* 1991, *28*(3), 195–201.

Mayo, E. *The Social Problems of an Industrial Civilization*. Cambridge, Mass.: Harvard University Press, 1945.

Moore, M., and Delworth, U. *Training Manual for Student Services Program Development*. Boulder, Colo.: Western Interstate Commission on Higher Education, 1976.

Morrill, W. H., Oetting, E. R., and Hurst, J. C. "Dimensions of Intervention for Student Development." *Personnel and Guidance Journal,* 1974, *52,* 354–359.

Napier, R. W., and Gershenfeld, M. K. *Groups: Theory and Experience*. (4th ed.) Boston: Houghton Mifflin, 1987.

Nisbett, R. E., and Wilson, T. D. "News From Groups." Institute of Social Research, University of Michigan, Summer 1978, 4–5.

Pace, C. R., and Kuh, G. D. *College Student Experiences Questionnaire*. (4th ed.) Bloomington, Ind.: Indiana University, 1998.

Perry, W. G., Jr. *Forms of Intellectual and Ethical Development in the College Years: A Scheme*. New York: Holt, Rinehart and Winston, 1968.

Schuh, J. H., and Upcraft, M. L. "Facts and Myths About Assessment in Student Affairs." *About Campus,* 1998, *3*(5), 2–8.

Strange, C. "Managing College Environments: Theory and Practice." In T. K. Miller, R. B. Winston, Jr., and Associates (eds.), *Administration and Leadership in Student Affairs.* (2nd ed.) Muncie, Ind.: Accelerated Development, 1991.

Suskie, L. A. *Questionnaire Survey Research: What Works.* Tallahassee, Fla.: Association for Institutional Research, 1992.

Upcraft, M. L., and Schuh, J. H. *Assessment in Student Affairs: A Guide for Practitioners.* San Francisco: Jossey-Bass, 1996.

Winston, R. B., Jr., Miller, T. K., and Cooper, D. L. *The Student Developmental Task and Lifestyle Assessment.* Athens, Ga.: Student Development Associates, 1999.

DIANE L. COOPER *is associate professor and coordinator of the student affairs administration doctoral program at The University of Georgia.*

SUE A. SAUNDERS *is assistant professor and coordinator of the college student affairs administration master's program at The University of Georgia.*

2

This chapter discusses the importance of determining learning domains, goals, and objectives, as well as the ethics of good programming. It provides an overview of different types of program delivery methods and of how knowing your audience affects the overall program and its direction. Finally, the chapter explores the importance of reflection in learning.

Developing Interventions That Focus on Learning

Debora L. Liddell, Steven Hubbard, Rochelle Werner

Programming, like any other activity that is taken on by a student affairs professional, should be intentional in order to be effective. But intentional toward what end? This chapter defines the assumptions underlying powerful programming and suggests ways in which programming can be linked effectively to student learning.

Assumptions of Powerful Programming

In order for programs to be effective, the following assumptions should be met.

Programming Can Be a Viable Vehicle for Transmitting Knowledge, Affecting Skills Development, Changing Attitudes, and Helping Students Reach Their Potential. This may be the heart of student affairs work and, indeed, the soul of the student affairs educator.

Programming Requires an Unwavering Commitment to Act Ethically. As we think about our role as educator-programmers, we assume a certain degree of power, authority, and influence that should be coupled with deep responsibility and commitment to keep students safe, even as we are stretching their limits. This means we do not incite groups for the purpose of a good discussion. We do not embarrass students for the purpose of making a point. We accept students where they are developmentally—the racist and the radical alike. Only then can we understand—and act upon—how best to reach them.

Programming Must Be Tied Explicitly to Learning. The Student Learning Imperative (American College Personnel Association, 1994) asks us to be mindful about integrating academic and out-of-class activities for the purpose of learning. In spite of our best efforts to plan for certain outcomes, we do not get to decide what students learn. This mandates that we be intentional in our efforts. There is no substitute for good, careful planning. In a similar vein, powerful programming should have outcomes that are measurable.

Powerful Programming Focuses on the Learner. There will always be political reasons to pursue programming. Perhaps a grant is tied to alcohol awareness efforts or a racial conflict in the residence halls leads to calls from members of the campus community for diversity programming. However, even the most externally driven efforts can be undergirded by good planning and clear learner-focused assessment; they can involve the students who are most affected by our efforts.

Powerful Programming Involves Those Most Affected. Although we may, as practitioners, bring a certain expertise about content, we learned long ago that students need to be invested in our efforts if they are to succeed. This requires that we pay attention to the needs of existing student groups, and even fringe groups, to make certain that we have not overlooked any of our constituencies.

The Act of Planning for and Implementing an Educational Program Is Research in Action. The tools necessary for this research in action include assessment and evaluation. In order for programming efforts to pay off, our work must be built on the foundation of good needs and outcomes assessment; otherwise, we have no way of judging the efficacy of our efforts.

Toward What End Should We Program?

When planning for and implementing educational interventions, the question at the center of programming should be: What do we want the student to learn?

Data generated from the Involving Colleges study identified five outcome domains of learning that students reported as a result of their out-of-class experiences. The outcome domains are: cognitive complexity, knowledge and academic skills acquisition, interpersonal competence, practical competence, and humanitarianism (Kuh, 1995). These domains can be used as effective starting points in our program planning.

What does it really mean to create a program that will enhance cognitive skills, interpersonal skills, or one's commitment to humanitarianism? Information in Table 2.1 examines the five domains of learning, their characteristics, and the primary factors that influence such learning.

Using Goals and Objectives

Once learning domains are established and the results of the needs assessments have been considered, the next step is to develop goals and objectives. A *goal* is what an individual is striving to accomplish, an overarching target or aim (Ender, McCaffrey, and Miller, 1979). Because of the general

Table 2.1. Domains of Learning

Desired Outcome Domain	Characterizations	Factors That Positively Influence This Outcome
Cognitive complexity	Reflective thinking Critical thinking Intellectual flexibility	Interaction with peers Involvement in academic activities Living-learning activities
Knowledge acquisition and application	Gains in knowledge Transferable academic skills	Academic activities Contact with faculty Leadership opportunities
Interpersonal competence	Self-awareness Autonomy Confidence Social competence Sense of purpose	Interactions with peers Leadership opportunities
Practical competence	Vocational competence Practical skills	Leadership opportunities Work Organizational activities that are work related
Humanitarianism	Altruism Aesthetics	Interactions with peers Leadership experiences

Source: Developed from G. D. Kuh, "The Other Curriculum: Out-of-Class Experiences Associated with Student Learning and Development." *Journal of Higher Education,* 1995, *66*(2), 123–155.

nature of a goal, evaluating or determining its completion may be difficult. This is why specific objectives will be effective for the program planner.

A well-written *objective,* which by nature is specific, helps us to decide when a goal has been accomplished. Generally a short statement that relates back to one of the declared goals of the program, an objective might describe one way in which the goal can be reached.

Very often, the setting of goals and objectives will influence the amount of motivation we have to reach them. The use of goals and objectives can help set clear standards for program planners and participants. If all of the individuals who are involved in the program planning have a part in setting the goals and objectives, the focus will more likely remain clear and group investment will more likely be maintained.

Accountability poses another compelling reason that goals and objectives are vital to program success. With clear goals and objectives set, the student affairs professional can be prepared and confident in explaining the department's actions. Most important, developing clear goals and objectives allows one to determine whether the effort was appropriate to the outcome.

Writing Goals and Objectives

A program goal is a general statement that is something observable and realistic, yet challenging to an audience. A goal is a desired end state. It provides the "what" of the program. It answers the question, What do we want to happen as a result of implementing this program? A goal is stated as a positive, occurs within a given time frame, and is attainable given the resources available.

Similarly, an objective is considered the "how" of the program. How are we to accomplish the specific goal? An objective is directly related to the goal; it describes a single result; it specifies a target date for accomplishment; it is realistic, attainable, and measurable. An objective answers the question, "How would the participants behave if the goal were achieved?"

Effective goals and objectives neither center on the program facilitator nor detail the content of learning. They do, however, focus on the learner, describing how the learner may be changed as a result of the program.

An example of a goal and objectives written for an interviewing workshop might look like this:

Topic: Interviewing for jobs
Learning domains: Practical competence, interpersonal competence
Goal: To develop interviewing skills to be used upon graduation from college
Objectives: Upon completion of the program, participants will
  be prepared to answer the most common interviewing questions
  be able to formulate questions to be asked of the employer in an interview
  identify their sources of anxiety about job interviews
  be able to research the company with which they are interviewing

Delivering Programs

Once general goals and measurable objectives are established for the program, consideration should be given to the design and delivery of the program. A variety of delivery systems are described next.

One-Shot Program. Although a program of short format may limit what students can learn, it can be all the time we have to work with. A program of this type is delivered in one to two hours and, as such, its objectives should be specific and realistic. The less time we have with a group, the less able we may be to deal effectively with affective and personal content issues. Appropriate topics would be informational in nature, for example, résumé writing, financial skills, and time management.

Ongoing Program Series. Programs delivered in this context allow the facilitator to take a longer view of learning. You can decide whether the group will be an intact one (all participants at all sessions) or one that drops in for each session. (A discussion of the implications of audiences follows.) In an ongoing program series, each session can have specific objectives that contribute to more general program goals. An example of this would be a series on building community with individual sessions on personal responsibility, civic participation, and how to establish healthy interpersonal community relationships.

Structured Workshops for Groups. Workshops, as opposed to programs, tend to be longer in duration, sometimes extending over a period of one or more days. The emphasis tends to be on the development of specific skills and typically integrates traditional instruction with practice of the skill. A two-day workshop, for instance, focused on developing leadership skills can be very effective in an off-campus setting. Sequestering participants captures their time and attention, increasing the opportunity for personal awareness, challenge, and growth. These opportunities are coupled, however, with increased responsibilities for logistical, physical, and ethical implications.

Ongoing Groups. Once considered the exclusive responsibility of the campus counseling center, programming targeted to ongoing groups was also once thought of as remedial or preventive in nature. However, effective program planners know that with ongoing groups, trust can be developed over time, allowing more risk taking by the participants. This setting, therefore, can facilitate learning that is more personal in nature. Learning can be extremely powerful in the context of peer groups. Ongoing groups can address issues and attitudes that developed over time; they can therefore require a longer-term commitment for the unlearning of those attitudes. These groups can range from appreciating diversity, making healthy choices, training in assertive behavior, or developing healthy relationships. Of course, remedial and prevention issues still lend themselves to ongoing groups—phobia-desensitization training, eating disorders, or anger management. These topics are typically facilitated by professionals specifically trained in mental health and physical health issues. An effective facilitator will ascertain through a needs assessment the necessary conditions for learning, allocating the time necessary to facilitate learning.

The topic of learning in groups is explored in more detail in Will (1997).

Consultation Programming. With the increased importance of learning partnerships with faculty and other educators, student affairs professionals have occasion to act as consultants about students and student life issues. You may be asked to provide training to those who serve students. This request may be to provide specific training, facilitate a solution-oriented discussion, or to help campus groups get along better. Unlike other relationships, when we act as consultants we leave our authority to solve the problem behind us and act only as the provider of information, the group processor. Participation in the consulting partnership is voluntary for both parties, and, regardless of your investment, the implementation of any advice you may offer is strictly up to the consultee. A particular issue of which to be aware when consulting is the potential for role conflict. The student affairs consultant is a visitor in someone else's house and, as such, should be knowledgeable of and sensitive to the norms and cultures of the host. This role requires that you do extensive homework regarding the problem and the intended audience in order to most effectively serve them. Of particular importance is the extensive interview prior to the consulting, during which you and the consultee pursue agreement on objectives, expectations, roles, evaluation strategies, and ethical concerns.

Passive Programming. The increasing demands on students' time mandates that we examine the importance of passive programming on our campuses. Anyone who has ever posted flyers on a student bulletin board knows that while we may lose some intentionality in our intended outcomes, we gain access to students in their worlds, allowing the program planner to reach the student in a somewhat random fashion but with a specific targeted objective. In that regard it is opportunistic learning. Effective passive programming can happen on the World Wide Web (an interactive Web site, a chat room, or a virtual pamphlet stand), in the residence hall lounge (guided chats following a provocative television show seen by residents), or even in public restrooms ("stall talk," tear-off resource sheets, newsletters). Programming of a passive nature can be cost-effective because it may require little staff involvement and even less financial resources.

Programming as a Function of a Student Affairs Unit. At a macrolevel, many student affairs units have developed broad guidelines and methods for the delivery of programs. Although student affairs units are not delivery systems per se, since any of the methods discussed earlier may apply, they nonetheless warrant an important consideration in programming. The programming philosophy, models, and procedures established by student affairs units may shape, to a large extent, the nature of cocurricular programming on campus. For example, student affairs units that subscribe heavily to using a wellness model of programming may, unintentionally, be steering the programming efforts more in the direction of one-shot programs or ongoing programming series, simply by adopting the wellness model. In order to ensure that all of the wellness dimensions are addressed in programming, wellness models may lead the programming efforts in the direction of shorter duration or one-shot programs. To be sure, there are plenty of exceptions where ongoing groups or lengthy workshops are devoted to wellness. Nevertheless, institutions should consider the ways in which larger philosophies and models of student affairs programming may affect specific program delivery system choices.

Knowing Your Audience

To be an effective facilitator of learning requires a commitment to know your learners. This is necessary because while you may have specific learning objectives, only the learners are in control of what they will take away from the program you are planning. Knowing the program audience requires that we understand what they know (an integral aspect of your pre-program assessment). Knowing the audience also requires that we identify and verify the assumptions we hold about our audience.

Effective facilitators understand the dynamic nature of learning and teaching. There is a fundamental difference between programming for an intact group (a Greek chapter, student organization, athletic team) and programming for a drop-in group (anyone is welcome).

The dynamics of an intact group may differ significantly from the dynamics of a drop-in group. This is especially true in terms of feelings of trust, belonging, sense of identity and purpose. In addition, the needs of each group may vary significantly depending on the history, traditions, and length of association of group members. Tuckman (1965), for example, highlighted the ways in which groups develop through a series of stages: forming, storming, norming, performing, and adjourning. The effect of a specific programming intervention with a group may be very different for one that is forming (newly established) as opposed to one that is norming (well-established, members of the group are working to full potential). In addition, we know through the work of Hershey and Blanchard (1977) that both groups and group leaders vary in terms of their focus on accomplishing tasks with the group or in establishing relationships. Both of these factors—level of group formation and task-versus-relationship behaviors of the group—play a significant role in terms of the way in which groups come to appreciate, learn, and understand any programming efforts. Effective programmers pay attention to the needs of their audience and set expectations appropriate to those needs.

Effective facilitators also know that not all instructional techniques are appropriate for all groups. Program planners should take care to ascertain the level of trust in a group, the level of risk assumed by participants, as well as the psychological and physical safety provided to learners. A general principle at work here is: the more didactic instruction is, the more impersonal and more external the learning can be. More didactic instructional strategies require low involvement, low disclosure, and low interaction with others. On the other hand, the more experiential an activity, the more personal and more internal the learning, the greater the self-disclosure, the more the interaction with others (Jones and Pfeiffer, 1979). For instance, a lecture is more external (and therefore less risky) to the learner than a role-playing exercise. Certainly role-playing can be fun—it is adaptable to a group and can allow participants a great deal of ownership. But because it tends to focus on the affective and cognitive sides of learning (that is, one's emotional self is just as present in role-playing as one's cognitions), participants can become too immersed; the roles can become too personalized; and therefore participants may feel too vulnerable for real and lasting learning to occur.

Effective facilitators bring more than planning skills to a program. They also bring a set of interpersonal skills, one of which is that they know themselves well. They understand their biases and work not to inflict those on participants; doing so surely retards learning and development. They understand the limitations of their training and the ethical responsibilities that accompany programming. They listen actively, suspend judgment, and accept the learner at whatever stage he or she may be. They follow basic principles of effective feedback: focusing on behavior and observations (what is said or done) rather than making inferences about the person (why something is said or done); describing concretely in the here and now rather than placing judgment in the abstract; focusing on sharing ideas and information rather than providing advice; considering the value and utility of the feedback to the receiver over its value to the feedback provider. Effective feedback should be specific ("That was an insightful response") as opposed to general ("Good job on that question"), and prompt.

Effective facilitators allow adequate time for discussing, challenging, and reflecting. In short, they know how to model, in front of the learning group, the kind of behavior they expect from the group: respect for others, support for others, honesty coupled with accountability, and an authenticity with self and others. They understand how to fulfill their professional ethical code in program planning, implementation, evaluation, and follow-up.

Sealing the Deal: Using Reflection Activities to Foster Learning

The act of reflecting on an experience is a vital step in the learning process (Dewey, 1933; Kolb, 1984). When reflection occurs, the learner internally observes and reviews the activity, then begins to create a personal meaning and understanding about the experience. The reflection process connects the concrete to the abstract (Hatcher and Bringle, 1997; Kolb, 1984) or creates a link between an activity and a meaningful learning experience.

The term *reflection* often describes both a cognitive process and a learning activity (Hatcher and Bringle, 1997). For instance, cognitive development theorists demonstrated that the process of reflection is essential in experiential learning programs. The process of reflection gives the learner a framework to make internal observations, extract ideas, synthesize information, and compare alternative meanings from certain activities (Alliance for Service-Learning in Education Reform, 1997; Gish, 1990; Kolb, 1984). In this description, reflection is considered process oriented and not outcomes or content based. Reflection is the incubation period to internally develop abstract concepts or ideas.

Reflection is also described as a learning activity that facilitates the learning process (Hatcher and Bringle, 1997). Some common examples of these activities include journal writing, discussion groups, e-mail, listservs, note taking, and many other activities.

In the learning process, conducting reflection activities produces many benefits. For example, reflection activities may alleviate internal contradictions, misunderstandings, or differences in interpretations (Dewey, 1933). Reflection activities also evaluate programs both for the learner and the instructor, supervisor, or program planner (Goldsmith, 1995). This evaluation can provide a productive exchange of ideas between the student and instructor to improve program implementation. In addition, students are able to receive feedback from themselves, peers, and others through these reflection activities.

The process of reflection also has been proven to have a positive effect on students' academic and personal development. For instance, in the area of service learning, Conrad and Hedin (1990) stated that the use of reflection in learning activities improved basic academic skills (reading, writing, and speaking), proficiency of subject matter, and ability to solve problems. The use of reflection also increased students' knowledge of the experiential learning process, and helped them become more proficient in connecting concrete experiences with abstract conceptualizations. In the area of personal development, Conrad and Hedin stated that the use of reflection in service learning programs increased students' self-awareness of their skill level, self-image, ideas about others, and career development. Through reflection, students were also able to empower themselves by taking the opportunity to reflect on their service experiences and the benefits they brought to others and themselves.

Mullins. In a study conducted by Mullins (1997), reflection activities were conducted to maximize learning from a class's involvement with a Habitat for Humanity building day. Thirty-two college students participated in this study and joined in reflection-discussion groups after completing the project. From the discussions, students learned that three important learning connections developed: institutional, conceptual, and interpersonal. Mullins discovered that institutional connections were developed between the educational institution, businesses, and nonprofit agencies. In addition, students grew in their interpersonal skills by connecting with each other, faculty, agency staff, and businesses. These interpersonal connections also increased respect for others, exploration of gender roles, and leadership skills. Finally, the use of reflection helped students connect theory to practice, as students gained a better understanding of the concepts explored in the class.

Hatcher and Bringle. To maximize learning through the use of reflection, Hatcher and Bringle (1997) developed five guidelines to use in experiential learning activities. These guidelines include linking the experience to learning objectives, providing guidance during the experience, scheduling regular reflective activities, allowing opportunities for feedback, and clarifying values.

The first guideline they present is linking the experience and activities to the learning objectives. The reflection activities must match what the program learning objectives plan to accomplish. For example, if the program learning objective involves job shadowing for the student to learn more about a specific career, writing a journal will help the student explore and reflect on those experiences. However, if one of the program's objectives is to encourage interaction within a group, journal writing may not completely accomplish the objectives of the program. A combination of writing a journal and participating in group discussions could be a useful reflection activity in this example.

The use of guided reflective activities is another guideline Hatcher and Bringle discuss. Providing guidance during reflection activities is extremely important to correct misunderstandings and misinterpretations. In addition, it can also help identify any stress or concerns that came up during the learning experience. For instance, some activities may create emotional distress for students. A reflection activity may help identify those problems; a professional could offer assistance or refer the student to the appropriate resource.

Hatcher and Bringle also encourage the use of regularly scheduled reflection activities to increase critical thinking. A regular schedule of reflection activities helps students become aware of the progress they completed from the beginning of the program.

Another guideline identified by these authors is that reflective activities should allow opportunities for feedback and assessment. Reflection can be very useful for program planners to learn more about their population, the effects of their programs, and the opportunities to improve the overall program. The student also benefits from self-assessment and feedback provided when completing reflective activities.

Reflection activities also provide an opportunity for students to clarify values (Hatcher and Bringle, 1997). Learning experiences often involve challenges to personal perceptions, contradictions to ideas, and risk taking. The use of reflection can help students identify their own values and provide opportunities to view them from different perspectives.

Reflection Activities

Many different activities maximize learning through reflection. All of the following activities encourage students to internally observe their learning experience and make the connections between theory and practice.

Journals.   There are many different types of journals, as pointed out by Goldsmith (1995) and Garmon (1998). Of course the most popular journals are personal journals, which include regular entries made by one student. However, there are also dialogue journals, team journals, and collecting journals. Dialogue journals are designed to give an opportunity for two people to exchange ideas. Team journals involve more than two people, giving participants a chance to take turns adding entries to the journal. Collecting journals is similar to creating a scrapbook with mementos from the learning experience.

Along with the many different styles of journals, many different ways are available to write journals. Some students have the tendency to write about the content of the experience instead of personal meanings, feelings, and perceptions they experienced. These journals become nothing more than a log of activities completed. To avoid this problem, Goldsmith (1995) suggests creating a list of questions for students to answer in their journals. In addition, students can write double entry journals that include two columns. In one column, students write down a list of activities they completed. In the other, students write down deeper feelings, perceptions, meanings, and internal observations they experience while completing the activity.

Group Discussions. To encourage group interaction and the development of interpersonal skills, small group discussions are an excellent way for students to reflect on a learning activity. Discussions give students a chance to challenge ideas and perceptions. They can also provide an opportunity for students to receive instant feedback while learning the process of group development.

As with journal writing, discussion groups should always include some type of framework to keep the conversation on topic. The best way to accomplish this is to create a list of questions for the group to answer. In addition, it is very important that the group facilitator be knowledgeable about the group development process.

Electronic Mail Lists or Listservs. E-mail journals and listservs provide a convenient forum in which to discuss and reflect on learning experiences. This electronic forum can encourage interaction and provide opportunities to discuss without requiring all members of a group to join in at a certain time or location. However, the facilitator must monitor e-mails and listservs to avoid miscommunication or the spreading of incorrect information. In addition, responses through electronic media can be slow if students or facilitators do not check their accounts regularly.

Case Studies. Before and after an educational experience, case studies provide an excellent opportunity for students to reflect on and experiment with unfamiliar situations. In this circumstance a case study presents a problem-based example. Usually, case studies create a safe environment to practice and plan for the learning experience. For instance, case studies are used in many training programs to develop new skills and increase self-awareness. As a reflection tool, case studies can also be used after a learning experience to provide time to review the experience and experiment with new ways to accomplish tasks.

In summary, activities used to foster reflective learning should have strong ethical underpinnings; activities should stretch the participant in engaging and stimulating ways, but they should be within the physical and psychological safety net that participants expect to encounter. Ground rules for discussion and challenge should be decided on and understood ahead of time. Activities should provide choices to participants and should help them make relevant and personal links to the facilitator's learning objectives. Finally, participants should honor the life experiences and the worldviews of colearners.

Conclusion

We presented in this chapter strategies for identifying and working from learning-focused goals and objectives. Strong and careful planning will enable program planners to evaluate outcomes. We have also presented information on different kinds of programming and discussed the dynamics present when presenting to certain audiences. Developing activities that require participants to identify what they have learned and how they might apply it will encourage the development of their critical thinking skills.

References

Alliance for Service-Learning in Education Reform. "Standards of Quality for School-Based and Community-Based Service Learning." *Social Studies,* 1997, *88*(5), 215–219.

American College Personnel Association. *The Student Learning Imperative: Implications for Student Affairs,* Washington, D.C.: American College Personnel Association, 1994.

Conrad, D., and Hedin, D. "Learning from Service." In J. C. Kendall and Associates (eds.), *Combining Service and Learning: A Resource Book for Community and Public Service.* Vol. 1. Raleigh, N.C.: National Society for Internships and Experiential Education, 1990.

Dewey, J. *How We Think.* New York: Heath, 1933.

Ender, S. C., McCaffrey, S. S., and Miller, T. K. *Students Helping Students: A Training Manual for Peer Helpers on the College Campus.* Athens, Ga.: Student Development Associates, 1979.

Garmon, M. A. "Using Dialogue Journals to Promote Student Learning in a Multicultural Teacher Education Course." *Remedial and Special Education,* 1998, *19*(1), 32–45.

Gish, G. L. "The Learning Cycle." In J. C. Kendall and Associates (eds.), *Combining Service and Learning: A Resource Book for Community and Public Service.* Vol. 2. Raleigh, N.C.: National Society for Internships and Experiential Education, 1990.

Goldsmith, S. *Journal Reflection: A Resource Guide for Community Service Leaders and Educators Engaged in Service Learning.* Washington, D.C.: American Alliance for Rights and Responsibilities, 1995.

Hatcher, J. A., and Bringle, R. G. "Reflection: Bridging the Gap Between Service and Learning." *College Teaching,* 1997, *45*(5), 153–158.

Hershey, P., and Blanchard, K. *Management of Organizational Behavior: Utilizing Human Resources.* Englewood Cliffs, N.J.: Prentice Hall, 1977.

Jones, J. E., and Pfeiffer, J. W. *The 1979 Annual Handbook for Group Facilitators.* San Diego, Calif.: University Associates, 1979.

Kolb, D. A. *Experiential Learning: Experience as the Source of Learning and Development.* Englewood Cliffs, N.J.: Prentice Hall, 1984.

Kuh, G. D. "The Other Curriculum: Out-of-Class Experiences Associated with Student Learning and Development." *Journal of Higher Education,* 1995, *66*(2), 123–155.

Mullins, B. K. "What Does Building a House Have to Do with Learning?" *International Journal of Lifelong Education,* 1997, *16*(3), 227–242.

Tuckman, B. W. "Developmental Sequence in Small Groups." *Psychological Bulletin,* 1965, *63,* 384–399.

Will, A. M. "Group Learning in Workshops." In J. A. Fleming (ed.), *New Perspectives in Designing and Implementing Effective Workshops.* New Directions for Adult and Continuing Education, no. 76. San Francisco: Jossey-Bass, 1997.

DEBORA L. LIDDELL is associate professor in the Division of Counseling, Rehabilitation, and Student Development at The University of Iowa, Iowa City.

STEVEN HUBBARD is assistant director for programming in the Henry B. Tippie College of Business at The University of Iowa. He works with the college's student organizations, the Prebusiness Learning Community, and first-year students.

ROCHELLE WERNER is a career consultant in eastern Iowa.

3

The authors examine the nature of programming partnerships between student affairs staff and others, including four case studies that highlight benefits associated with these partnerships.

Partnerships in Programming: Relationships That Make a Difference

Ann C. Highum, Jon P. Lund

Partnerships in programming is not a new topic. Anyone who has been involved in programming knows how important it is to forge relationships with a wide variety of constituencies that can help develop, shape, contribute to, and improve the types of programs we offer for students. But developing strong programming partnerships has taken on greater urgency. This is primarily due to the increased focus by student affairs staff on the way in which we may directly contribute to gains in student learning. We know, through an ever growing body of research (Ender, Newton, and Caple, 1996; Kuh, Douglas, Lund, and Ramin-Gyurnek, 1994; Pascarella and Terenzini, 1991), that the out-of-class environment holds great promise for increasing student learning and growth if that environment is properly shaped. However, fostering powerful out-of-class learning environments is a difficult task and takes the efforts of a large number of individuals working together. Nowhere is this more succinctly stated than in the Joint Task Force on Student Learning's document *Powerful Partnerships: A Shared Responsibility for Learning.* "People collaborate when the job they face is too big, is too urgent, or requires too much knowledge for one person or group to do alone. Marshalling what we know about learning and applying it to the education of our students is just such a job. . . . only when everyone on campus—particularly academic affairs and student affairs staff—shares the responsibility for student learning will we be able to make significant progress in improving it" (1998, p. 1).

Since learning is both an individual and a social activity, it only makes sense that we form partnerships with others in helping to foster even greater learning. And this partnership, as the Joint Task Force suggests, holds promise for also helping us in our learning. Through the process of collaboration, we ourselves grow as we come to better understand the perspectives and contributions of those engaged with us in the collaborative process. Thus we model for our students the social dimensions of learning.

The purpose of this chapter is to highlight the ways in which programming partnerships between student affairs staff and others may lead to powerful relationships that make a difference for students. The chapter begins with a brief overview of the types and nature of programming partnerships. Then, four programming partnerships representing various institutional types are highlighted. Each of these partnerships illustrates the way in which creative programming partnerships may make a difference for students. The chapter ends by summarizing the most important aspects, as embodied in the examples, that led to success in each of the partnerships.

Types of Partnerships

Programming partnerships on college and university campuses come in many shapes and sizes. In general, they can be categorized roughly into four areas: partnerships within and among student life units; partnerships with academic affairs offices and faculty; partnerships with offices, departments, and units outside of academic affairs; and partnerships with constituencies off campus. Obviously, one other very important group with which student affairs staff frequently form partnerships is students. Because of the natural and historic relationship between students and student affairs staff members around issues of programming, collaborative efforts with student groups are not addressed below. Suffice it to say that this is one of the most important groups with which we must continue to forge strong partnerships if we truly want to make a difference for students in terms of their learning and personal development.

Developing strong programming partnerships with others is not merely a good idea, it also makes a great deal of sense from a practical perspective. Partnerships with all of the constituency groups mentioned above help to focus and expand programming resources, especially in terms of personnel, money, expertise, and creative ideas. In addition, programming partnerships position colleges and universities to better meet the needs and expectations of students, thereby helping them more fully realize the benefits of their education. It is through collaborative efforts that the barriers preventing seamless learning begin to fall (Joint Task Force, 1998; Terenzini, 1999).

Of the partnerships listed, the one receiving perhaps the most attention has been the relationship between academic and student affairs. A general theme has permeated the writing on this topic: student affairs must strive to develop structured, collaborative efforts with academic affairs (Brown, 1990; Reger and Hyman, 1989; Ryan, 1989). Although the general theme has been consistent, opinion about the actual motivation for the collaboration varies widely. Reger and Hyman (1989) argue that the motivation is that collaboration improves the image of student affairs; Brown (1990) and Ryan (1989) that collaboration is educationally sound in that it enhances the development of the whole person; Kuh, Shedd, and Whitt (1987) that collaboration is a natural process that may or may not occur and results from similarities between the shared goals of student affairs and liberal education.

More recently, researchers also have focused on describing the nature of the relationships between higher education institutions and their communities. Many institutions have a long tradition of disassociation from the communities within which they exist (Goodman and MacNeil, 1999). Indeed, many higher education institutions, especially those that are heavily residential in nature, have structured campus environments that function much like cloistered communities. Instead of encouraging an outward focus on the community, these institutions turn inward, effectively closing off collaborative efforts with those in the community. This is not the case for all institutions, with community colleges being a notable exception. Nonetheless, colleges and universities across the country increasingly are realizing that they are indeed interdependent with the communities in which they are located (Goodman and MacNeil, 1999). As a result, establishing strong partnerships around programming—in areas such as service learning, internships, cultural performances, and others—has become important for many colleges and universities.

Model Programming Partnerships

The case studies that follow describe different kinds of college and university programs and projects that we identified and believe to be of value in illustrating strong programming partnerships between student affairs staff and other constituencies. Although the descriptions are brief, we believe they highlight the important aspects of each partnership that resulted in the programs' success. We have intentionally included summaries of programs, detailing different types of relationships at distinct types of institutions.

The Wellness Program at Wheeling Jesuit University. Wheeling Jesuit University is a small residential Jesuit institution located in rural West Virginia. The university enrolls fifteen hundred graduate and undergraduate students, with approximately eight hundred students (most of them undergraduate) living on campus. Founded in 1954, the institution is the newest of the twenty-eight Jesuit universities in the United States. The university's mission and daily work reflect heavily on its Jesuit roots; the president is required to be a member of the Jesuit order and several members of the faculty are also Jesuit.

In the late 1980s, the dean of students at the institution created a wellness program for students. The program was created in order to better meet the perceived need by many on campus that the institution had to do a better job of educating students about health and wellness issues and encouraging them to lead healthier lives. From the beginning, the focus of the program was on helping students to become acquainted with wellness concepts, develop skills and abilities reflective of healthy lifestyles, and come to appreciate the importance of wellness in one's life, both on and off campus.

Although conceived in the dean of students' office, many of the early programs were developed to facilitate physical education programming using funds secured from outside sources. Once the wellness-related programs were developed (many of them by faculty members), the decision was made to request faculty action in making student attendance at wellness programs a requirement for graduation. The faculty eventually approved this unique aspect of the wellness program. The requirement has become a cocurricular graduation requirement at Wheeling Jesuit University, not an academic requirement.

Unique aspects of the current wellness program include:

Faculty and staff from virtually all areas of the campus, assisted by students, develop and offer programs that address eight wellness dimensions. Unless an individual is brought in from outside the university to present on a specific topic, presenters receive no compensation for their participation.

Students are required to attend two programs from each of the eight areas at some point during their college career.

Often, programs are paired with a particular course so that faculty members may encourage student attendance by offering extra credit.

A member of the student affairs staff coordinates all wellness program offerings. Records on student participation are kept and used to monitor completion of the cocurricular requirement.

A few obstacles initially presented challenges for development of the program. Perhaps one of the most serious was the perception by some members of the university community that the wellness program would compete with the academic experience for students' time. In addition, the time spent in developing these programs took time away from other faculty activities. Even though there was strong opposition to the wellness program requirement when first approved in 1989, the program gained significant support on campus so that it easily passed its reevaluation vote in 1991. By 1991, most faculty viewed the program as one that enhanced student learning outside the classroom, rather than as a threat to the academic experience inside the classroom.

The program's early success was due in no small part to the relationships its director fostered with others on campus. These relationships helped to move the program forward and win over dissenting voices along the way. The program also flourished due to the partnerships formed between the student affairs staff, faculty, and other staff involved in the program. The culture of Wheeling Jesuit University also contributed to the program's success. The institution's strong ethic of service meant that the vast majority of programs could be presented by individuals who volunteered their time, thus ensuring the cost-effective delivery of a significant number of programs. Finally, the program succeeded because it allowed students a great deal of choice in how they would fulfill their cocurricular wellness requirement, with 250 program options each year.

The First-Year Experience at Wartburg College. Wartburg College, a small residential Lutheran college in Waverly, Iowa, is an institution of approximately fifteen hundred students, with over 80 percent of its students living in college residence halls. The college's mission places emphasis on nurturing and challenging students for lives of leadership and service, and the faculty and staff take their role in helping to ensure student success seriously. Rewards for faculty are based on teaching and service, especially out-of-class contacts with students.

In early 1990, Wartburg College developed a first-year student experience. The program grew out of a strong partnership between the vice president for academic affairs and the vice president for student life. The two vice presidents had developed a solid working partnership and had discussed the idea of a first-year student program as a way to help increase the retention rate for first-year students. With the help of faculty members, they developed a noncredit course and piloted the course with a small group of new students. The first-year experience designers believed the most promising parts of the course, in terms of increasing student retention, were those activities that addressed the transitional concerns of first-year students and more intentionally connected faculty members with students outside the classroom. Although the course held great promise initially, the proposal to make it a credit-bearing course was not approved by the faculty. The programming aspects of the course were continued, however, and the components are now coordinated by a faculty member. The current program's primary focus remains relatively unchanged from the initial purpose: to provide the maximum amount of interaction between faculty members and students in both structured and unstructured settings. Activities include:

Faculty-led small group discussions, on books selected by faculty, during new student orientation.
An optional program involving student participation in a low ropes challenge course. Follow-up discussion by faculty members focuses on college transition issues.
Evening "knight" workshops (the Wartburg team mascot is the knight) in residence halls, which are developed and implemented by the first-year coordinator and residence hall staffs. The workshops are held during the first eight weeks of the semester.
Case studies provided by the faculty chair of ethics in which students, in residence hall floor groupings, read about and discuss issues that often impact first-year students.

Required foundation courses that focus on community-related issues. Each
student must take at least one of these courses during the first year and
may earn course points by attending community events (for example,
convocations, artist events, "knight" workshops).

From the program's inception, the college president was interested in
and committed to developing support from across the college community
for the program. This top-down approach provided a sense of institutional
commitment for the program. In addition, outside funding provided a rev-
enue source to support resources and incentives to formulate and test new
efforts.

In spite of the president's active support for the program, faculty members expressed commitment to the out-of-class programming aspects of the
effort, but did not believe the course merited awarding academic credit. The
faculty vote not to award academic credit for the first-year experience came
despite data from pilot sections indicating a higher retention rate and grade
point average for students in the course.

Across campus, faculty members and other staff have developed a
deeper appreciation of the transition needs of first-year students. Aspects of
the program have seeped into the language on campus, so much so that the
term *first-year experience* is now a part of the fabric of the institution as well
as part of the language in written pieces for prospective students.

The SKILL Program at the University of San Francisco. The University of San Francisco (USF) is an urban Jesuit institution located in
downtown San Francisco. The campus has an enrollment of thirty-five hundred undergraduate and twenty-five hundred graduate students. Most of the
students at the institution are commuter students, with only first-year students living on campus. Like other Jesuit colleges, USF's mission is based
on Jesuit ideals, and many of its students, including a significant portion of
international students, are graduates of Catholic high schools.

The SKILL program for students was developed as a joint venture
between the student affairs staff, other staff, and faculty at the institution.
The program encourages students to complete a series of activities and projects in the following areas: service (S), knowledge of self in relation to others (K), integrity (I), literacy (L), and linkages (L). Programs across these
categories cover everything from personal responsibility statements for students (integrity) to workshops on obtaining internships (linkages). The various activities in which students may participate are drawn from existing
program options, as well as from newly developed activities that fit into
these categories. The various initiatives, begun in 1998, were conceived as
a series of opportunities that would encourage commuter students to
develop deeper and more meaningful connections to the university.

The effort was initially championed by a faculty member in the business department who served concurrently on two different advisory com-
mittees that were struggling with ways in which to help commuter students

become more involved in and connected to the institution. He suggested that the various staff and faculty get together to discuss their respective efforts, which he saw as having considerable overlap. Once the program was established, he began to explore ways to integrate the SKILL program into his courses. Currently, students in his database management courses are developing software that will track student participation in the program and allow them to easily record their activities and progress for use in portfolios and résumés.

One of the major obstacles in implementing the SKILL program was the existence of what one person at USF described as "pillars" on campus. People in the various offices, units, and departments were all doing great things but often in isolation from one another. The SKILL program encouraged partnerships that crossed artificial office barriers and required program developers to communicate more intentionally with one another. Although this has been positive for the institution, it has not come about without some difficulty. The program has fostered a greater degree of information sharing and partnerships across the institution, and the data generating efforts will lead to timely feedback for students and a convenient mechanism to assess the effectiveness of the program.

The Cooperative Education Program at Scottsdale Community College. Scottsdale Community College (SCC) is a large two-year college of approximately ten thousand students, located on an Indian reservation bordering Scottsdale, Arizona, on the east side of the Phoenix metropolitan area. Its students come from a wide variety of backgrounds, encompass the spectrum of age ranges, and have a diverse set of goals for their college education. The very nature of the community college is one in which the college "partners" with its community. This notion is so important at SCC, in fact, that the president often states, "Community is our middle name." The college's underlying philosophy is to serve its community by serving its students, that is, to match its services and programs to students' needs and goals. Its occupational programs provide an interesting example of strong community programming partnerships. Through advisory councils made up of individuals from local businesses, health facilities, and industries, the college obtains valuable information that is used to better prepare students for entry into the workplace and the larger community.

The cooperative education program was enhanced in 1992 with federal Title VIII grant funding. The goal of the program is to help students get on-the-job training related to their career objectives. The program either matches students with employers for work experiences in their major area, or allows students currently in jobs to formulate new, specific learning objectives through which they develop new skills for academic credit.

Over the past seven years, the program director has focused intentionally on developing a large network of employer contacts in the community. Students are matched with employers and paired with faculty members from the college. Students, employers, and faculty members then work together to establish specific learning objectives related to the partnerships. Faculty members and the program coordinator track students throughout the semester and evaluate the attainment of the learning objectives at the end of the experience. In addition to work on-site with the employers, students also are required to attend seminars on work-related topics sponsored by the program's advisory council.

Several challenges were encountered during the implementation phase of the program, all related to the ways in which the program would be marketed. First, the program coordinator had to acquaint faculty members with the goals and objectives of the program and the potential value of the program for students. She also had to get faculty members to endorse the cooperative education concept. Second, the program coordinator had to establish networks of employers and supporters from the Cooperative Advisory Council, the Chamber of Commerce, and through other college employee contacts. Third, she had to communicate the value of this work experience to students and gain their commitment for the program.

A major factor in the program's success rested in the solid initial contacts established with members of the community related to the goals of the program. Community partnerships helped to drive its implementation. In addition, as the community relationships solidified, faculty members became more interested in and supportive of the program's goals. The advisory council was another major reason for the program's success. Council members served as a solid core of supporters and helped to promote the program through the early phases of implementation. The advisory council's efforts on campus were acknowledged by a broader audience in 1998, when the State Council on Vocational Education recognized it as the best advisory council in Arizona.

Summary and Conclusions

The four case studies, each in its distinctive way, clearly demonstrate the ways in which partnerships help not only to enhance programming efforts on college and university campuses but also contribute to creating a better learning environment for students. Across the case studies, several themes emerge that highlight programming components that help to ensure success.

In most programming efforts, relationship building lies at the heart of successful initiatives. In the case studies presented, collaborative relationships were fostered and cemented by a belief in the positive benefits of the relationships for students and their learning. Successful programs find ways to transcend departmental or unit boundaries, help build trust and understanding among participants, and draw on the talents of all individuals who may be able to contribute to a better program. To be sure, this is an ideal situation and may not easily be attained on many campuses. Issues of territoriality, eventual ownership of the program, and the program's fit into the institutional culture are important considerations. This is true in all relationships and certainly noticeable in the collaborative partnerships between academic and student affairs staff. As two of the case studies alluded to, programming initiatives that also include an academic, credit-bearing component may become particularly problematic for the relationship. Nonetheless, successful programming requires partners to resolve differences and move forward with efforts to implement the program.

All of the case studies highlight another important component for success. Programming partnerships require an investment of resources, energy, commitment, and administrative support. All of these issues play a significant role in programming. As mentioned in the case studies, some programming efforts are aided by external funds, which simplify this part of the programming equation. Others receive staffing allocations or the vocal support of the president in order to move the efforts forward. What is clear is all programming efforts require some level of commitment of resources. The commitment of resources, however, is not in itself sufficient. A significant amount of money and staff time may be devoted to the success of a program, for example, but if the program does not meet student needs or does not reflect the culture of the institution, then the ultimate success of the program is questionable indeed.

Finally, successful programming takes time. The case studies illustrate the ways in which programming efforts evolve over time. This is especially true since relationship building is not a quick process. In addition, the nature or focus of programs may change as they are revised or directed by new individuals, as new goals are substituted for old goals, and the characteristics and needs of students and other stakeholders shift. What is often needed most, and frequently forgotten, is a modicum of patience and a long, sustainable vision for the final programming product.

References

Brown, S. "Strengthening Ties to Academic Affairs." In M. Barr, M. L. Upcraft, and Associates (eds.), *New Futures for Student Affairs: Building a Vision for Professional Leadership and Practice.* San Francisco: Jossey-Bass, 1990.

Ender, S., Newton, F., and Caple, R. (eds.). *Contributing to Learning: The Role of Student Affairs.* New Directions for Student Services, no. 75. San Francisco: Jossey-Bass, 1996.

Goodman, A., and MacNeil, C. "Collaborating with Our Communities." *About Campus,* 1999, 4(3), 19–24.

Joint Task Force on Student Learning. *Powerful Partnerships: A Shared Responsibility for Learning.* Washington, D.C.: American Association for Higher Education, American College Personnel Association, National Association for Student Personnel Administrators, 1998.

Kuh, G. D., Douglas, K. B., Lund, J. P., and Ramin-Gyurnek, J. *Student Learning Outside the Classroom: Transcending Artificial Boundaries.* ASHE-ERIC Higher Education Report No. 8. Washington, D.C.: George Washington University, 1994.

Kuh, G., Shedd, J., and Whitt, E. "Student Affairs and Liberal Education: Unrecognized (and Unappreciated) Common Law Partners." *Journal of College Student Personnel,* 1987, 28, 252–259.

Pascarella, E., and Terenzini, P. T. *How College Affects Students.* San Francisco: Jossey-Bass, 1991.

Reger, M., and Hyman, R. "Academic and Student Affairs: Perceptions on Partnerships." *NASPA Journal,* 1989, *26,* 64–70.

Ryan, E. "The Whale and the Elephant: A Fable for Our Time." *NASPA Journal,* 1989, *26,* 70–76.

Terenzini, P. T. "Form Follows Function. Right?" *About Campus,* 1999, *4*(2), 2–3.

ANN C. HIGHUM is vice president and dean for student life at Luther College in Decorah, Iowa. She has served for the past twenty-three years in various student affairs roles across a variety of institutional settings.

JON P. LUND is assistant dean for student life at Luther College, Decorah, Iowa.

4

Program implementation is a task-oriented process. This chapter highlights details to consider for effective program delivery and offers suggestions for dealing with unexpected circumstances that may arise throughout the course of a program.

Programming: Nuts and Bolts

M. Celine Hartwig

The successful delivery of any program depends upon thoughtful attention to details. Attending to details provides an avenue by which program goals and objectives can effectively be communicated. Undoubtedly, those of us who have been in the student affairs profession for a number of years can recall those moments when the unexpected happened in programs we attended or presented. Student government executives became angry regarding controversial assertions put forth by the presenter; staff members appeared disinterested and trickled out of the room shortly after the start of a professional development session; or looks of confusion graced the faces of a group of resident assistants following a lengthy explanation of a complex training exercise. Regrettably, most programmers can recollect the mishaps of those programs we attended or presented, the unforeseen flaws in the facility or presentation, or a presenter's shortcomings that consequently diminished, and possibly even sabotaged, the learning outcomes the program planning team had hoped for.

In Barr and Keating's (1985) model of program development, the program context, goal, and plan are equal components in the program development process. We must pay equal attention to each interdependent component in order to attain program success. Primary to that success is a well-planned, well-organized program and a consistent and polished presentation. This chapter specifically addresses the details necessary to implement programs, either one-time activities with a planned purpose and target population, or a series of planned interventions developed for a defined target population or to fulfill a specific purpose (Barr and Cuyjet, 1991). Additionally, this chapter offers practical points, or the nuts and bolts of programming, and discusses suggestions on handling difficult and unexpected circumstances.

NEW DIRECTIONS FOR STUDENT SERVICES, no. 90, Summer 2000 © Jossey-Bass Publishers

The Task Timeline

Having defined clear program goals and objectives and decided upon an approach, the program planning team is ready to set into motion the details of implementing the plan. The planning team's first assignment is to develop and delineate an appropriately detailed, comprehensive timeline reflecting all tasks to be accomplished, by when, and by whom. Include the proposed program date, time, and location once these details have been decided, as well as regularly scheduled planning meetings and locations, with each team member receiving modified timelines as needed. Although the timeline is an important tool for keeping the group focused, it must also be flexible enough so that the plan can be modified if the content is not accurately addressing or pinpointing program objectives, or if tasks cannot realistically be completed in the time allowed.

A team member or support staff member should summarize meetings and promptly distribute minutes throughout the program implementation and evaluation phases. All too often this simple yet important strategy for keeping members informed is either overlooked or underused. Minutes assist team members in accomplishing assigned tasks, remind team members who is responsible for completing which tasks, assist with accountability among team members, and serve as a historical document useful in program planning, review, and evaluation.

Time and Space

The success of a program may depend largely upon the time chosen to implement the program. Although the planning team may feel compelled to schedule a program based on room or speaker availability, it is important to first consider the availability of the target audience, and even more important, competing campus activities. Programming for students can be tricky, and investigating the timing of popular or upcoming campus or community events, holidays, standing student group meetings, daytime and large evening class schedules, exam schedules, and campus traditions is valuable. Program planners should check directly with the offices or student groups responsible for their own events and meeting schedules.

Implementing a program in an unfamiliar facility can present an assortment of problems that may reflect poorly on the presenters and damage the credibility of the event. Planners and presenters must familiarize themselves with features of the facility to ensure smooth program delivery. Similarly, the room must be a good fit for the design of the program. A discussion of campus safety issues with a group of resident assistants in a warm lounge with overstuffed chairs and dim lighting after lunch can be the demise of even the most dynamic program. When choosing a room the planning team should consider the following questions (not an exhaustive list):

1. Access—Will the building or door to the room be open in time for early arrivals? Is the room accessible to students with disabilities? Are there physically distracting aspects of the room?

2. Location—Is the room close or easily accessible to the target audience? Is it easy to find? Is parking available? Is the room labeled appropriately? Is the signage appropriate? Do participants need privacy? If so, is a more private room available?

3. Size—Is the room large enough for the number of participants expected to attend? Is it too large?

4. Equipment—Are there blackboards with chalk or whiteboards with markers? Is the room equipped with an overhead projector, video projection unit, slide projector, or screen? If not, is equipment available? Are there enough electrical outlets in the room? Will an extension cord be necessary? Is the temperature controllable?

5. Furniture—Are there tables and chairs? Are they movable? Is there an adequate number? If not, are more available? Are the chairs comfortable? Is a podium or table available for the presenter?

6. Lighting and sound—Are the light switches easy to access? Are there dimmers on the light switches? If so, are the controls easy to use? Is a technician needed? Does the room have a sound system that needs to be turned off? Is a microphone available? If so, is it the right type?

If the planning team is hosting the program outdoors, it should consider the previous questions, as well as reserve an alternate location in case of rain or choose an alternate rain date. The team should have a well-defined plan of action for moving a program to a rain location or for rescheduling a program. The plan should include who makes the decision to move or cancel the program, at what time the decision will be made, and how team members, the speaker, and participants will be notified. Failure to plan can lead to confusion and frustration for both the planning team and potential participants.

Campus Policies and Procedure Related to Programming

Throughout the course of implementing a program, it is important for members of the planning team to follow policies and procedures set forth by the institution where the program is taking place. In some cases, this may take a significant amount of investigation and time, particularly if the program is the first of its type on campus. Policies may even be developed as a result of the inquiry about the program. College or university operations manuals, policy books, division guidelines, and department manuals are all helpful resources; a majority of this information may be available on the institution's Web site. Many colleges and universities have policies with regard to reserving space, promotion and solicitation of events, negotiating and signing contracts, requiring insurance for large-scale events, health and safety issues, purchasing food and beverages from off-campus vendors, corporate sponsorship, and transporting students, staff members, and guests in vehicles.

Planning teams should become familiar with their institution's financial and budgetary policies. It is best not to be surprised by complicated or restrictive policies that might hinder the planning process or possibly prevent a program from taking place. By speaking with appropriate campus officials and using written resources, team members can ensure that all guidelines and procedures have been followed. Departmental business officers, personnel in the accounts payable office, personnel in the student activities office, account clerks, and departmental secretaries can all provide insight and guidance.

Promoting the Program

Effective promotional materials are well designed, free from errors, and state or imply the benefits participants will receive if they attend. The planning team should choose the program title carefully so that it piques interest and accurately reflects what will happen during the course of the program. A poorly titled program can lead to unrealistic expectations and disappointed attendees. In addition to including the program title, date, time (both beginning and ending), and location and speaker information, the planning team should be aware of institutional requirements regarding deadlines, size limitations of promotional materials, and requirements concerning information that must be included on materials in order to have them approved for posting, such as program sponsor(s), the institution's disability statement, or equal opportunity statement. Policies also may exist regarding the placement or use of commercial logos. For example, the University of Iowa requires that a flyer be no larger than eleven by seventeen inches and include both a sponsor's name and disability clause before it receives approval to post in residence halls. It is also a good idea to include either a name of a person or an office and a phone number so that interested persons have a point of contact for more information.

Although posters and flyers are standard promotional tools around college campuses, their effectiveness will depend on their placement and their ability to attract potential attendees' attention. When used in appropriate locations, folded paper table tents may be more effective than flyers because students take the time to read and discuss their content over meals or study sessions. Other effective promotional strategies include sending invitations or personalized e-mail to potential attendees, using target audience listservs, placing ads in the campus or local newspaper, listing the program in the newspaper events column, and promoting the event in departmental newsletters and at building information kiosks. In some instances the planning team may ask participants to register for a program in advance. This allows the planning team to monitor attendance and, if necessary, conduct more targeted marketing (*Guide for Colleges and Universities*, 1998). To stimulate enthusiasm for the program, planning team members should also talk about the program with selected individuals who can assist with promoting the program and identifying meetings at which program announcements can be made. It is very important, however, to know and abide by campus solicitation policies and procedures; failure to do so can mean setbacks in getting the word out.

Program Delivery Preparation

When choosing a presenter, the planning team should consider a presenter's ability to speak effectively and facilitate discussion; they should choose someone they have heard themselves or who has been recommended by colleagues. Other questions to consider include: Is the speaker controversial? Does the speaker make a good first impression and appear knowledgeable? Is the speaker able to give clear and specific directions to simulations and activities? Is the presenter skilled at redirecting discussion if it wanders? Has he or she presented the program before, or will he or she conduct a pilot program? Previous presentations and pilot programs assist the programmer in evaluating weakness in program content, design, and presentation skills.

A program presenter or facilitator cannot achieve program goals without getting a clear sense from the planning team of what he or she is supposed to accomplish. A presenter may be an expert on a particular topic, but without a clearly defined purpose, program goals, learning objectives, or a plan to implement those goals and objectives, neither the presenter nor participants will understand the direction in which the program is headed (Goad, 1982). Chapter Three of this volume provides detailed information about ways to successfully delineate a program implementation plan. All those involved should meet with presenters at least once to discuss what is expected. Additional topics of discussion are the appropriateness of activities such as simulations, role-playing, and interactive exercises, as well as the presenter's written materials and facilities requests.

Prior to the program, the planning team or presenter should assemble a programming "tool box"—a box of supplies that may be needed for the program presentation. Include a variety of objects that can assist the programmer in a minor emergency. Tape, scissors, a stapler, pencils and pens, paper clips, additional handouts, transparencies, chalk, markers, name tags, and tissues are all standard fare. An extension cord, a three-pronged plug adapter, backup disks and slides, additional supplies, and any other relevant equipment accessories should also be included. Finally, include an additional copy of the program outline, program evaluation forms, room and equipment confirmations, and, if applicable, copies of official agreements or contracts.

Developing Program Materials

The average person can hold approximately five key points in his or her working memory at once (Kearney, 1996), and a common mistake that inexperienced presenters make is either to put too much information on a visual aid or to make the print too small for participants to read. Powerful visual aids assist people in grasping main points quickly. Whether the presenter is using a computer screen, overhead projections, or a flipchart, visual aids must be simple and clear. Effective visual aids use key words, have a significant amount of white space, alternate colors, use clear text, and list a maximum of five ideas on each page (Kearney, 1996).

Similarly, programmers can enhance learning by providing important points of reference or helpful information in program handouts. Handouts should include: (1) page numbers, even if there are only two; (2) headers and footers—include the title, date, and section name of the handout in addition to the page number; (3) white space, which helps participants easily locate information, signals a change in content or focus, and provides space for taking notes; (4) a variety of fonts to help draw attention to particular words or phrases or emphasize importance; and (5) headings and subheadings, to emphasize levels of importance (Petit, 1994).

Getting Started

Prior to the program, the presenter should have a clear understanding of who will be in attendance and the roles they play within their institution. Nothing is more frustrating than attending a program conducted by a facilitator who is confused about the participants' level of education, profession, or their official titles. For example, referring to a group of professional hall directors as students or a group of community college students as kids will immediately extinguish any credibility the presenter may have established. On a similar note, addressing a topic too simplistically or too technically may be insulting to the attendees. A quick, on-the-spot assessment of participants' abilities and backgrounds can assist the programmer in redirecting program content to effectively achieve program goals and objectives.

To engage participants, the introduction should be well-rehearsed, well-timed, and efficiently executed; this sets the tone for the remainder of the program. The programmer would do well to commit opening remarks to memory. A rough beginning can derail the presenter, particularly if participants' initial verbal and nonverbal reactions reflect a lack of confidence in the presenter and a sense that the remainder of the program may be mediocre at best. Unfortunately, participants can be quick to judge, which can compromise the presenter's presentation and undermine the success of the program. The program introduction must be well planned and include the following: (1) a brief introduction of the presenter; (2) a statement of what the presenter intends to accomplish throughout the course of the program (goals and objectives); (3) a program outline and time frame; (4) ground rules and expectations for participation; (5) housekeeping items such as location of restrooms and availability of refreshments; and (6) plans for evaluation. The more prepared the presenter is to deliver the program introduction, the more likely he or she is to stay on task and effectively work within the schedule as the program progresses.

Functions of the Facilitator

It is the facilitator's role to establish program direction, to set clear expectations and provide ground rules for participation, and to establish appropriate time frames for learning activities and discussions. By establishing clear, positive group expectations for behavior at the onset and then modeling those behaviors throughout the course of the program, the facilitator helps participants know how to conduct themselves. The facilitator should also closely monitor the participants' energy levels and suggest breaks when necessary. Controlling the pace of the program keeps participants engaged and alleviates boredom (Silberman, 1990).

More important, however, is the facilitator's role as the individual who holds participants responsible for their own learning and behaviors. Facilitators can be successful in doing so by consistently and actively observing program participants throughout the course of the program and then responding accordingly. In other words, the facilitator should gather accurate information about how participants are relating to the materials as well as to the other participants and the presenter, and then appropriately intervene to clarify the content of the material or the program process (Friedman and Yarbrough, 1985). By clarifying discussion points, providing feedback and insight, and varying the program length, content, and learning methods, the facilitator helps enrich participants' learning experiences. Of course this implies a certain amount of flexibility. The facilitator must be prepared with a variety of ways to proceed. Understanding that group demographics, education levels, and reasons for attending the program (for example, mandatory versus optional, personal interest in the topic) affect group dynamics which, in turn, affect group learning is also important to consider. The effective use of facilitation skills allows the facilitator to actually focus on participant learning and the content of the program when addressing difficult situations rather than focusing on the problem that has just arisen. These points are detailed in Chapter Two.

Program Follow-Up

Program planning teams make the common error of devoting an inadequate amount of attention to the evaluation process and to follow-up tasks. This is understandable given the magnitude of time and energy devoted to the program assessment, development, and implementation processes. But program planners place the future of the program in jeopardy when they fail to solicit and analyze relevant information in order to fashion appropriate modifications and establish future plans. Chapter Six of this volume details a thorough examination of the program evaluation process.

Compile a comprehensive program file following the program evaluation process and include the following: (1) the names and titles of planning team members; (2) needs assessment information and results, including relevant resources on the program topic; (3) a list of resource consultants; (4) the task timeline; (5) the meeting minutes; (6) the marketing strategy and copies of all marketing materials; (7) the name and title of the presenter; (8) copies of handouts; (9) a program outline; (10) a copy of evaluation materials and an evaluation summary; and (11) copies of financial paperwork and any official university documents. Planning team members also should send thank you notes and include a summary of the program evaluations when appropriate.

Expecting the Unexpected

Primary to achieving program success is for participants to perceive the presenter as skilled, intelligent, and credible. Taking time to think about unexpected situations that may arise increases the presenter's ability to attain program goals and assists the presenter in appearing polished and in control. Difficult questions from attendees or unexpected facilities and equipment concerns can all be managed with a little forethought. Preparation will help a programmer think quickly and react appropriately, and will decrease the likelihood of the presenter becoming flustered, embarrassed, or angry. McArdle (1993) even goes so far as to suggest that the programmer generate a list of areas within the program that might provoke questions, generate a list of questions that might be asked in those areas, and then write out and practice responses.

Should the presenter behave differently if a reporter from the student newspaper is in attendance? What if a participant falls asleep or disrupts the program with jokes or a distracting habit? Table 4.1 provides possible responses to potentially problematic, "what if" circumstances that may arise throughout the course of a program. While a limited number of "what if" sit-

Table 4.1. "What If" Situations and Potential Responses

Situation	Response
Participants do not participate in discussion	Wait; give participants time to answer.
	Reword question or restate assigned task for clarity.
	Ask nonthreatening, noncontroversial questions.
	Place participants in small groups to discuss questions.
	Instruct participants to write answers and share with group.
One participant dominates the discussion	Acknowledge participant's input.
	Ask participant to hold comments so that others can share their thoughts.
	Ask other participants for their input.
	Do not call on a participant directly.
	Explain to the group how remainder of time will be spent.
	Let participants know when questions will be taken.
Participant is disruptive	Ignore the disruption if it is not too distracting.
	Pause; make eye contact with the participant until disruptive behavior stops.
	Use negative facial expressions.
	Privately ask participant to refrain from disruptive behavior.
	Walk toward or stand near disruptive participant.
	Place hand on participant's shoulder.
	Ask the participant a question.

Table 4.1. "What If" Situations and Potential Responses (cont'd)

Situation	Response
Participant asks difficult or controversial question	Acknowledge difficult or controversial nature of question.
	Ask other participants for their thoughts.
	Choose words carefully; state what is known about the topic.
	Admit what you don't know.
Equipment fails	Check all equipment ahead of time.
	Use on-site technician when available.
	Have written operational instructions available.
	Use available resources (whiteboard, chalkboard, paper and markers).
	Prepare handouts.
Only two or three people attend	Modify or eliminate program activities.
	Personalize the program.
	Ask participants what they hope to gain.
	Engage participants in conversation.
	Join the participants around a small table for an intimate discussion.
Participant becomes argumentative	Acknowledge the value of the participant's view; show interest.
	Ask other participants for their opinion.
	Agree to disagree.
	State what is agreed upon; then state what is disagreed upon and why.
	Remain calm; avoid a power struggle.
Twice as many people come as are expected	Only allow all to attend if attendance does not compromise the quality of program.
	Modify program activities, simulations, or assign observers when appropriate.
	If necessary, limit number of participants.
	Offer another program to participants.
Participant becomes visibly distraught	Take a break.
	Privately speak with participant; ask how to help.
	Express concern.
	Provide appropriate referrals.
The room is double-booked	Bring appropriate confirmation information.
	Bring a copy of publicity.
	If another program is in progress, politely interrupt and speak with presenter.

uations are addressed in the table, the presenter and planning team would do well to brainstorm additional situations prior to program delivery.

When encountering "what if" situations, a programmer should be nothing less than fair, impartial, and respectful of participants. Behaving in a professional and dignified manner, using humor appropriately, and ensuring confidentiality when discussing sensitive issues are all essential practices. Creating an environment that is potentially hurtful or damaging to participants, even if this is not the intent of the programmer, can have a negative and long-lasting impact on the participants. This not only damages the trustworthiness of the programmer, but also calls into question the reputation of the student affairs office he or she represents.

Belittling or arguing with participants or appearing frustrated can damage a presenter's credibility and leave participants feeling uncomfortable, which may sabotage learning. Remain calm and polite at all times; avoid power struggles at all cost. In some instances the best course of action when dealing with a problem participant is to do nothing. If the problem behavior recurs, often other participants will make it known that the behavior is inappropriate or distracting. Preventing difficult situations through brainstorming potential problems, then thinking about ways to intervene will assist the programmer in establishing and maintaining control as well as allow the presenter to focus on the program itself rather than the difficulties that might occur.

Conclusion

Program preparation takes time, forethought, and practice, and the program implementation process is rarely linear. In fact, the planning team may be accomplishing several tasks at once, and tasks may be changing based on feedback and review. The program implementation checklist in Exhibit 4.1 serves as a chapter summary and can be used as a practical planning tool when thinking through the details of implementing a program.

Exhibit 4.1. The Program Implementation Checklist

❑ Develop a Detailed, Comprehensive Task Timeline
  __ define and assign tasks
  __ set task deadlines, including program date and time
  __ meet regularly
  __ summarize meetings and distribute notes
  __ update task timeline as needed

❑ Choose a Time and Place
  __ consider availability of target audience
  __ investigate timing of campus events
  __ consider campus calendar, holidays, and class schedules
  __ consider location, room size, and accessibility
  __ consider equipment and furnishings
  __ develop a contingency plan for outdoor programs

Exhibit 4.1. The Program Implementation Checklist (cont'd)

❑ Investigate Campus Policies and Procedures Related to Programming
   __ check appropriate written resources
   __ consult appropriate campus officials

❑ Develop and Distribute Promotional Materials
   __ choose accurate and engaging program title
   __ develop targeted promotional strategy
   __ investigate campus solicitation and distribution policies
   __ select promotional methods
   __ develop materials
   __ distribute materials

❑ Prepare for Program Delivery
   __ investigate speaker possibilities
   __ choose and meet with speaker
   __ clearly articulate goals and objectives
   __ discuss program content
   __ assemble "tool box"
   __ conduct pilot program

❑ Develop Program Visual Aids and Materials
   __ create simple, clear handouts and visual aids
   __ review for content accuracy
   __ proofread for grammatical and spelling errors

❑ Prepare for Unexpected Situations
   __ brainstorm potentially difficult questions and situations
   __ brainstorm responses
   __ bear in mind ethical considerations

❑ Starting the Program
   __ gain understanding of participants and their needs
   __ plan and prepare the introduction
   __ memorize program introduction

❑ Facilitating the Program
   __ establish program goals and objectives
   __ set clear expectations and ground rules
   __ prepare appropriate learning activities
   __ monitor participants and respond accordingly

❑ Program Follow-Up
   __ conduct appropriate evaluations
   __ compile comprehensive program file
   __ write thank you notes

References

Barr, M. J., and Cuyjet, M. J. "Program Development in Student Services." In T. K. Miller, R. B. Winston, Jr., and Associates (eds.), *Administration and Leadership in Student Affairs*. (2nd ed.) Muncie, Ind.: Accelerated Development, 1991.

Barr, M. J., Keating, L. A., and Associates (eds.). *Developing Effective Student Services Programs: Systematic Approaches for Practitioners*. San Francisco: Jossey-Bass, 1985.

Friedman, P. G., and Yarbrough, E. A. *Training Strategies from Start to Finish*. Englewood Cliffs, N.J.: Prentice Hall, 1985.

Goad, T. W. *Delivering Effective Training*. San Diego, Calif.: University Associates Publishers and Consultants, 1982.

Guide for Colleges and Universities: Conducting and Marketing Business Training Programs. Alexandria, Va.: PBS Business Channel, 1998. Videotape.

Kearney, L. *Graphics for Presentations: Getting Your Ideas Across*. Menlo Park, Calif.: Crisp, 1996.

McArdle, G.E.H. *Delivering Effective Training Sessions: Techniques for Productivity*. Menlo Park, Calif.: Crisp, 1993.

Petit, A. *Secrets to Enliven Learning: How to Develop Extraordinary Self-Directed Training Materials*. San Diego, Calif.: Pfeiffer, 1994.

Silberman, M. *Active Training: A Handbook of Techniques, Designs, Case Examples, and Tips*. San Diego, Calif.: University Associates, 1990.

M. CELINE HARTWIG *is assistant to the director and conference coordinator for the Department of Residence Services and an adjunct lecturer in the Division of Counseling, Rehabilitation, and Student Development at The University of Iowa, Iowa City.*

5

Program evaluation is a critical step in effective program planning. The programmer needs to know whether and how students change as a result of educational experiences. Through a systematic collection of data, the programmer gathers evidence of how programs help students meet their learning objectives and fulfill institutional goals. Further, the results of program evaluation can inform the next program planning cycle.

Knowing What Works: Program Evaluation

Margaret A. Healy

How do you know that the program or workshop you just offered to students has made a difference for them? Does the program accomplish the stated objectives? How can you make your program more effective? When you offer a variety of programs to accomplish the same objective, how can you measure which one is the most effective? When deciding which programs you will continue to offer and which will be dropped, what evidence do you provide to support your recommendation? The purpose of this chapter is to help planners find answers to each of these questions. Doing so is the basis of effective program evaluation.

What Is Program Evaluation?

It can be difficult to differentiate between research and program evaluation. Certainly program evaluation and research have common elements, including careful design, systematic data collection, the use of quantitative and qualitative research methodologies to analyze data, and the need to communicate the results. However, program evaluation differs from research in one important way. As Worthen and Sanders (1973) explain, "*Evaluation* is the determination of the worth of a thing. It includes obtaining information for use in judging the worth of a program, product" (p. 19). In contrast, "*Research* is the activity aimed at obtaining generalizable knowledge . . . which may result in theoretical models, functional relationships, or descriptions[,] . . . obtained by empirical or other systematic methods and may or may not have immediate application" (p. 19). The results of program evaluation are intended to be used for decision making while research results are intended to be used for theory building and description, which may not have any immediate use.

Program evaluation is intended to provide evidence that permits programmers and decision makers to make judgments about the program. Hanson (1978) identifies five basic requirements for evaluating program effectiveness. First, program evaluation is theory-based; the programmer may choose from several models and theories of program evaluation to guide the development of the program evaluation design. Second, good program evaluation assesses a program's effectiveness and efficiency. Third, sound research methodologies are required for good program evaluation. Fourth, good program evaluation requires that the results be communicated. Finally, program evaluation is decision-oriented. This is perhaps the most distinctive difference between program evaluation and research. The results of program evaluation are used to make decisions about the program.

Worthen and Sanders (1973) suggest there are two types of program evaluation, formative and summative. In a formative evaluation, the researcher gathers evidence to support the ongoing development and improvement of a program. For example, the results of the program evaluation for an alcohol education program may demonstrate that the participants are not able to correctly identify the civil and criminal charges for underage possession, underage consumption, and driving while intoxicated. The planners decide to revise the components of the program that provide this information. The programming unit uses the evaluation results to modify the program. Therefore, using formative evaluation, the programmer is the decision maker.

On the other hand, summative evaluation provides evidence for external decision makers—perhaps department heads or other institutional officers—who will determine whether the program should be continued, augmented, reduced, or terminated. Summative evaluation has a feedback process that goes outside the programming unit. For example, the vice president may question whether an alcohol education program makes a difference in students' use of alcohol. The programmer is asked to present the results of the program evaluation so the results may be considered when deciding whether to eliminate, continue, or expand the alcohol education program.

Although the data collected may be the same for formative and summative evaluations, the presentation will differ. Whether the results are used within the programming unit or outside it, the evidence collected is intended to be used in decision making.

The Context for Planning Programs and Their Evaluation

How do student affairs units decide what programs they should develop or sponsor? Planning occurs within an institutional context and is guided by student needs assessment, the institutional mission and goals, and the theory that guides the programmer's understanding of the student's educational experience (Andreas, 1993).

The institutional mission and goals provide statements of what is important to the institution. They also supply insights into those factors that decision makers for programs consider important, and help define the commitments to students who attend. The mission and goals for the college or university frequently become more focused for student affairs staff through the adoption of student affairs or departmental mission and goals statements. Programmers should keep these priorities in mind when making choices about programs (Lyons, 1993). When a program is evaluated, one critical issue will be whether the program supports the institutional mission and goals. Most institutions will not continue to put resources into programs that are not related to these and to desired student outcomes.

Finally, the programmer must use theory to determine in what ways students need to learn and grow. Theory will undergird what the program entails and how it is designed.

Acquisition of Knowledge, Skills, and Values or Attitudes

In order to design a useful program evaluation, the programmer must define the program objectives. On what assumptions are they based? Who is the target audience for the educational intervention and how will the desired outcome be manifested? Will the program be effective if one or more of the individual participants is different, or will a group of individuals need to change in order for the program objectives to be reached? Is the program designed to facilitate developmental change? Is the program intended to change the environment or culture of the organization? Although the program audience will be individual students in every case, the program impact may be measured in multiple ways: the change may occur in individuals or it may be measured only for the group. The desired student outcomes and target audience for the program will guide the design of the program evaluation and the interpretation of the data collected.

Typically, educational interventions are intended to change students' knowledge, skills, or attitudes. Once a programmer knows how students are likely to change, then it is critical to state how the change will be measured. The objectives must be specific and measurable and should define the outcomes students will obtain from participating in the program. How will students be different?

Knowledge. Some programs are planned on the assumption that students need to acquire knowledge about an issue in order to change their behavior. Thus, when students have sufficient knowledge they will better understand the issue and will be more likely to make more informed choices. When designing an alcohol education program, for example, the objective may be to increase students' knowledge about the effects of alcohol use and misuse and to change the way in which students consume alcohol.

The assumptions and programming objectives suggest what evidence should be collected for the program evaluation. If the program objective is to increase students' knowledge about alcohol, then a simple paper-and-pencil test at the beginning and end of the program could provide evidence on how students' knowledge about alcohol increased over the course of the program. In order to determine how long the participants retain their new knowledge, the programmer may choose to ask participants to complete a survey one week or one month after the conclusion of the program. If the program is effective, students will likely have greater knowledge about the effects of alcohol. To gain a full picture of the program's impact, however, it is important to test the assumptions that were made at the outset of the program as well. Therefore, a second part of the program evaluation might collect data about students' alcohol use before and after they participated in an alcohol education program.

Skills. If the program objective is to teach or improve the participants' skills, how will the programmer measure the impact of the program? For example, for a workshop to teach new student organization treasurers how to set up the organization's books and how to use the institution's services for treasurers, the skills the programmer is attempting to develop are very measurable. The evidence may be collected from staff members in the office that provides financial services to student organizations. Are the books set up properly? Do they balance? Are paperwork and financial documents completed properly and on time? The evaluation of the effectiveness of the treasurer's training program may be measured through the process of doing the student organization's regular business.

Other skills are not quite so easily measured. One of the objectives of a leadership development series may include developing the skills needed to run an effective meeting. Among the skills taught is how to set an agenda. The student's agenda-setting skills may be assessed when the adviser reviews the agendas for meetings with the student leader. However, the mere fact that the student leader develops excellent agendas does not mean that a meeting will run well. Obviously, setting agendas is only one of the many skills a leader must acquire in order to run an effective meeting. Furthermore, other members of the group must possess sufficient skills to fulfill their obligations to the group and overall group effectiveness.

The acquisition of certain skills may not come about easily or quickly. Indeed, the student may need to develop a repertoire of skills in order to improve overall performance. A student leader may need to master a cluster of skills before he or she is able to be a more effective leader. So a program evaluation might aim to capture the development of an entire skill set from a series of educational interventions, rather than the development of a single skill that may or may not be affected by a single program. At the beginning of a term of office, for example, an adviser may meet with the student leader to identify what skills the leader needs for effective leadership.

The student leader may identify that she needs to acquire skills in agenda setting, parliamentary procedure, leading team-building exercises, and managing debates. After the student leader participates in leadership workshops, the program evaluation may require the adviser to observe her and provide feedback on the four skills the student leader identified.

Some changes require that more than one person acquire or develop the needed skills before there can be measurable change in the performance level of the group. The programmer should understand when and how new skills will result in change in performance for an individual or a group. When all group members must develop skills in order for them to function more effectively, it may be appropriate to present the program to them as an intact group. When working with a student organization on conducting effective meetings, the programmer may ask the group to define the characteristics of a successful meeting. At the conclusion of each meeting, the group may take time to review the characteristics and evaluate which characteristics were present. These data may be used by the leaders to determine how to structure the next meeting. In addition, the data may be provided to the adviser and the programmer as evidence for the program evaluation. The members also may be asked to evaluate their contribution to creating a successful meeting and their use of key skills taught in the leadership development workshops. These data may be used as individual results or may be reported solely at the group level.

Attitudes. Some programs are intended to change students' attitudes or perspectives about issues; these objectives can be difficult not only to accomplish but to measure. A program may have objectives to create positive attitudes toward diversity among the participants. The programmers assume that students must change their attitudes before they can change their behavior. Evaluating a program that is intended to change attitudes brings with it several challenges. First, it is frequently obvious to students what the "right" perspective or attitude is. Thus, they may treat any pre- and post-test evaluation as a knowledge test, and give the answers they know the presenter is seeking, regardless of their own attitudes. Second, students' attitudes are shaped by their environment, family, friends, and faculty, and it is unlikely that a single program may have the same impact as the messages students receive day after day. Furthermore, students may change their behavior without changing their attitudes for the purpose of conforming to conduct codes governing intolerant or biased behavior. Thus, when an objective is to change how students perceive situations and issues, evaluation of students' perceptions provides a substantial challenge.

Designing the Program Evaluation

Components and goals of effective evaluations are discussed next.

Taking the Program's Measure. A program evaluation should measure how students have changed after participating in the program. What do they know now that they did not know before? What can they do that they could not do before? From what new perspective do they now view the world? The knowledge, skills, and attitudes students acquire through programs lie at the heart of the program evaluation. How are students different? Under what conditions is change most likely to occur? How long does the change last?

A program evaluation should also answer questions that help measure how the program can be different and better. Were students satisfied? Would they recommend that other students participate in the program? Were all the examples presented and educational activities used productive for the participants? What did the participants like best? What did they like least? Another question to ask in a program evaluation is "how can this program be improved?" Each of these questions assist the student affairs professional, as a programmer and an educator, in enhancing the program design in order to make the program more effective for the next audience.

Another important use for program evaluation is to provide the programmer with feedback about the program's design as well as about the presenter's facilitation skills. The program evaluation may shed light on the presenter's performance and suggest areas in which the presenter may wish to improve.

Components of the Design. The components of the program evaluation design begin with the learning objectives. Next, the programmer identifies the direct and indirect ways that change or learning should occur. Then, using basic research design strategies, the evaluator will determine the hypotheses, the instruments, the subjects, and the methods for collecting and analyzing the data. Like good research, a program evaluation is planned prior to program delivery. Finally, the programmer may serve as the evaluator or he may enlist a colleague as the evaluator.

Hypotheses About How Students Have Changed. In addition to asking participants to assess the program, the evaluator may also want to identify indirect measures of the program impact. Are students who participate in an alcohol education program less likely to be sanctioned through the judicial process for misuse of alcohol? Are student organization treasurers who participate in a program about the institution's expectations of their role less likely to have problems keeping the organization's books?

Effective programming may also result in a direct and inverse relationship between the program and student behavior. For example, a program about sexual assault may result in an increased number of reports of sexual assault. It may indeed be the case that the total number of incidents of sexual assault on campus has remain unchanged, but as a result of the program, students may now feel more comfortable in reporting the behavior.

Strategies for Data Collection. There are a number of strategies for collecting data about the impact of a program. A standard program outline may include an overview of the objectives of the program, an introductory exercise that is intended to help the group become familiar with both the topic and the other participants, one or more educational activities (for example, an experiential activity, a mini-lecture, completion of a self-assessment), and a closing activity.

🌶 One strategy is to include in the program design a closing activity, which may become part of the program evaluation. One of the more common closing activities is to ask each participant to state one important thing they learned from the program. This permits the participants to reflect actively on what they have learned from the program and to make meaning out of the educational activities they have just completed. An alternate closing activity is to ask participants to develop a contract for new behavior, that is, to determine one thing they will do based on what they learned in the program.

There are several ways to use the contract concept. The facilitator may ask the participants to share their plan with one other person in the group and then ask them to follow up with their partner a short time later. Or the facilitator may ask the participants to write their plan on a piece of paper and place it in a self-addressed envelope so that the facilitator may follow up at a designated time. When the closing activity is part of the program evaluation plan, the facilitator should be certain to record the lessons learned or the types of behaviors specified in the contract in order to have the data for any written program evaluation.

🌵 A second strategy for collecting data is to ask participants to complete a paper-and-pencil evaluation of the program at the conclusion of the program. A simple instrument that requires a limited amount of time to complete is best. This method of collecting data may be most effective for groups that have come together for only a single program (for example, students who attend a résumé workshop in the career development center). An on-the-spot evaluation can be effective and yield the best response rate.

On the other hand, when the membership of the group will change over a period of time, it may be best to collect data about the effect of the program a few days or weeks after the program ends. In order to effectively evaluate the program at a later date, the evaluator must know who the participants are and how they may be reached. This method may be most effective for intact groups that have regular meetings (for example, a residence hall floor or a Greek chapter). Again, a simple paper-and-pencil instrument may provide sufficient feedback. When designing a program evaluation that will lag after the program ends, the evaluator must balance the need to measure the long-term impact of the program with the possibility that other events or educational experiences may also influence the knowledge, skills, or attitudes the program was intended to change.

🌱 A third strategy for collecting data about the impact of a program is to follow up with the participants face to face, either asking them how they used what they learned in the program or observing the participants while they apply the skills. This method is obviously time-consuming, and the utility of the data collected should be commensurate with the time invested in its collection.

Tools for Measuring Change in Students. A single program can help students learn important knowledge, skills, and attitudes. The programmer may be able to document, through effective data collection, what the participants have learned. Most of the tools for measuring change, such as Winston, Miller, and Cooper's (1999) Student Developmental Task and Lifestyle Inventory or Pace and Kuh's (1998) College Student Experiences Questionnaire, will not consistently capture small changes in students. Therefore, the design and process of program evaluation becomes very important.

Reporting the Results. Good program design provides the means for collecting data that can be used and reported for program evaluation. When used for formative evaluations, data provide evidence that permits the facilitators and administrators associated with the program to continue to refine and modify it so that it accomplishes its objectives more effectively.

Student affairs administrators will also regularly ask questions about the best use of resources in serving students. To answer this question, decision makers may have to examine in a summative sense all programs and services provided in order to determine the right mix to meet student needs and fulfill institutional obligations. When gathering evidence to respond to this question, decision makers and programmers will be comparing program evaluations in order to make decisions about continuing programs.

For both formative and summative evaluation, program planners will be called upon to report on the results of their programs. Communicating the results is a crucial step in the programming process, a step that is sometimes overlooked.

The program evaluation report is very different from a research report. The evaluator may write up the results of the student data collection in a traditional research report. That report might include a statement of the program objectives and assumptions, the hypotheses about change in students, the research methodology, psychometric properties of the instrumentation, the descriptive and inferential statistics, and the conclusions made based on the data presented. However, this research report should never stand as a program evaluation report. The program evaluation report has a very different purpose and a different audience.

The audience for a program evaluation report is decision makers. The program evaluation report must be written with the needs of the decision makers in mind, including an understanding of the context within which decisions will be made (Brown and Podolske, 1993). The decision makers may or may not be knowledgeable about the program topic or strategies for creating student change. Thus, it is important the program evaluation report be nontechnical and free of jargon. After reading the program evaluation, the decision makers will act. The program report must provide the evidence in a manner that will permit the reader to understand the program's fit with institutional goals and student needs, the intended and unintended outcomes, and the evaluator's recommendation, if requested or expected. The program evaluation should be short and simple, typically no longer than two or three pages, perhaps accompanied by tables and documents that provide further information for those who are interested.

Conclusion

Program evaluation is a critical element in the programming cycle, for it permits the programmer to close the loop between the conceptualization and delivery segments of the program planning process. The program evaluation provides evidence about how students may have changed, highlights whether or not the intended outcomes were accomplished, and provides suggestions on how to improve the program. When program evaluations are used in the aggregate, they can become part of an outcomes assessment program as well. When program evaluations are coupled with other measures or indicators, they may provide valuable insights into the way in which students grow and change as a result of the total educational experience at the institution. The results of program evaluation and outcomes assessment may then be used to shape future programs or change departmental mission and goals.

Program evaluation is a basic skill for every programmer. And program evaluation is an essential ingredient in effective program planning and management.

References

Andreas, R. E. "Program Planning." In M. J. Barr and Associates (ed.), *The Handbook of Student Affairs Administration*. San Francisco: Jossey-Bass, 1993.

Brown, R. D., and Podolske, D. L. "A Political Model for Program Evaluation." In M. J. Barr and Associates (eds.), *The Handbook of Student Affairs Administration*. San Francisco: Jossey-Bass, 1993.

Hanson, G. R. "Conclusions and Further Resources." In G. R. Hanson (ed.), *Evaluating Program Effectiveness*. New Directions for Student Services, no. 1. San Francisco: Jossey-Bass, 1978.

Lyons, J. W. "The Importance of Institutional Mission." In M. J. Barr and Associates (eds.), *The Handbook of Student Affairs Administration*. San Francisco: Jossey-Bass, 1993.

Pace, C. R., and Kuh, G. D. *College Student Experiences Questionnaire*. (4th ed.) Bloomington, Ind.: Indiana University, 1998.

Winston, R. B., Jr., and Miller, T. K., and Cooper, D. L. *Student Developmental Task and Lifestyle Inventory Manual*. Athens, Ga.: Student Development Associates, 1999.

Worthen, B. R., and Sanders, J. R. *Educational Evaluation: Theory and Practice*. Belmont, Calif.: Wadsworth, 1973.

MARGARET A. HEALY *is vice president for student affairs at Minnesota State University, Mankato.*

6

This chapter presents examples of good practice and what works in diversity programming. Practitioners must consider multicultural competencies for themselves and their students as well as the issue of free speech.

Programming for Multicultural Competencies

Mary Howard-Hamilton

Our college campuses have become an amazing tapestry of diverse student populations that bring with them a mélange of values, philosophies, and cultural traditions. Student affairs associations have addressed these shifting demographic trends over the course of the last decade. Accordingly, programs and activities have been designed to make the campus environment less hostile and more accessible to students of color and to educate as well as sensitize nonminority populations. Student affairs administrators and graduate preparation program faculty have made a concerted effort to promote diversity efforts both in and out of the classroom. The academic community requires programming that will move beyond the theme of tolerance by providing border-crossing and boundary-expanding experiences for everyone (Stage and Manning, 1992; Wilson, 1996). The purpose of this chapter is to review resources for and examples of effective diversity programming, and to suggest multicultural competencies for program planners and their students.

Several reports have concluded that diversity education is a flawed process on many college campuses (McEwen, Roper, Bryant, and Langa, 1990; Stage and Manning, 1992). However, some campus strategies have been successfully implemented in installments with partial support from upper-level administrators. The interventions developed to assist students of color were (1) special orientation programs for students of color and their parents, (2) mentoring by faculty and administrators of color, (3) formation of minority group organizations to provide coalitions and networking opportunities, and (4) encouraging students of color to join mainstream activities (Stage and Manning, 1992).

Although these efforts were an effective beginning, they did not address the most grievous and complex institutional problems underlying multiculturalism. Specifically, (1) the programs assumed that the students of color must adapt to the environment, thus placing the burden to change on students of color; (2) faculty and staff of color, who typically are outnumbered, overworked, and overwhelmed on predominantly white campuses, were being held responsible for the transition of students of color; and (3) the dominant culture was not receiving multicultural education (Stage and Manning, 1992). All student affairs administrators and preparation program faculty must become vigilant in their efforts to restructure and refine the old multicultural paradigm so that diversity initiatives and multicultural competencies become infused throughout the campus environment.

The American College Personnel Association and the National Association for Student Personnel Administrators (1997) developed seven core principles for good practice in student affairs, including a mandate to build supportive and inclusive communities. The seventh principle further elucidates that "Student learning occurs best in communities that value diversity, promote social responsibility, encourage discussion and debate, recognize accomplishments, and foster a sense of belonging among their members. Good student affairs practice cultivates supportive environments by encouraging connections between students, faculty, and student affairs practitioners" (p. 5).

Without the multicultural knowledge, skills, and awareness first and foremost as part of one's belief system there is a high probability that diversity programming may fail. This kind of learning is personal in nature and does not end. A multiculturally competent professional understands the need to be open to lifelong learning on diversity issues.

Multicultural Competencies and Good Practice

A unified curricular and cocurricular effort should exist between administrators and faculty so that discussions can take place regarding the psychosocial and intellectual development of college students. This combined curricular and cocurricular approach is not only important and effective for learning in general but is also effective for developing more multiculturally competent students (Howard-Hamilton, Richardson, and Shuford, 1998). The academic and administrative units cannot function in isolation from each other in this endeavor. Thus, "if institutions are to work from a holistic perspective, then there must be some agreement on what outcomes they hope students will achieve as well as what knowledge, skills, and attitudes a college-educated person should possess" (Howard-Hamilton, Richardson, and Shuford, 1998, p. 9). To encourage and strengthen one's sensitivity to diversity issues, a set of attributes elaborating upon the knowledge, skills, and attitudes students and faculty should develop to become culturally competent are noted in Table 6.1.

Table 6.1. Attributes of a Culturally Competent Student

	Knowledge	Skills	Attitudes
Awareness	Knowledge of self as it relates to your cultural identity	Self-reflection	Pride within your own cultural group
	Knowledge of other cultures and how they are similar or different from your own cultural group	Ability to identify similarities and differences across cultures and the ability to articulate that with others	Being different is okay
Understanding	Knowledgeable about issues of oppression and the effect it has on different cultural groups	Ability to see things from multiple perspectives	Discrimination due to one's cultural status is unjust
	Knowledgeable about the interactions between multiple oppressions such as race, gender, class, lifestyle, and religion	Understands difference in multiple contexts	
Appreciation/ Valuing	Knowledgeable about elements involved in social change	Able to challenge acts of discrimination	One must take risks in life social change
	Knows the effect cultural differences can have in communication patterns	Ability to communicate cross-culturally	Cross-cultural interaction enhances the quality of one's life

Source: From M. F. Howard-Hamilton, B. J. Richardson, and B. Shuford, B., "Promoting Multicultural Education: A Holistic Approach." *College Student Affairs Journal,* 1998, *18*(1), 5–17. Reprinted with permission from the *College Student Affairs Journal.*

Students, administrators, and faculty should work together to use these competencies when developing cocurricular and curricular student learning initiatives (Howard-Hamilton, Richardson, and Shuford, 1998). These attributes can be incorporated into successful programming if the practitioner models the appropriate behavior when teaching others about multiculturalism. Following are some of the behaviors that the culturally competent programmer could model:

- Is comfortable with and understands own racial-ethnic identity
- Is comfortable with own cultural identity(ies)
- Understands own biases

- Checks assumptions
- Is willing to ask questions about diversity
- Suspends judgment
- Understands the limits of own expertise
- Consults with students
- Sets a climate for dialogue, disagreement, reflection, challenge, and support
- Develops realistic leaning goals and objectives
- Follows up with students
- Enrolls in multicultural courses or workshops regularly
- Shares ideas and issues with a multiculturally competent mentor

Student affairs professionals should be prepared to effectively address diversity issues. Several characteristics "[help] student affairs professionals understand the range of behaviors and attitudes necessary for multicultural competence" (Pope and Reynolds, 1997, p. 270). They placed these characteristics in three nonhierarchical categories: awareness, knowledge, and skills. Specifically, a practitioner or educator does not have to master the abilities in one category before moving to the next. Pope and Reynolds further state that "Multicultural awareness consists of the attitudes, beliefs, values, assumptions, and self-awareness necessary to serve students who are culturally different from oneself. Multicultural knowledge consists of the information individuals have about various cultures. Multicultural skills allow for effective and meaningful interaction such as seeking consultation as necessary with people who differ from them culturally (p. 270).

In a recent study, King and Howard-Hamilton (2000) collected baseline data on the multicultural competency levels of graduate students at selected programs for the preparation of college student personnel. Results indicated that respondents rated themselves highest for multicultural awareness and lowest for multicultural knowledge. In other words, the students are aware that cultures other than their own have a differing set of beliefs. However, they did not acquire this information or knowledge through a structured educational process such as courses in African American or women's studies. Simply being tolerant of others may be relatively easy if there is no challenge to this process in either the classroom or workshop. However, engaging in a scholarly exploration of other cultures is not a simple undertaking because many programs do not require an individual diversity course within their curricula.

A candid and thorough personal evaluation of one's level of multicultural competence is paramount in programming so that one does no harm when working with diverse student populations (Howard-Hamilton, Richardson, and Shuford, 1998; King, 1999; Pope and Reynolds, 1997). Thus, it may be necessary for student affairs practitioners to "consciously prepare themselves for their role as educators" (King, 1999, p. 9) by taking additional coursework in academic areas that specialize in multicultural populations, for example, women's studies, African American studies, sociology, or anthropology. This would assist them in understanding the historical and political struggles of these diverse populations. An enhanced knowledge base of various cultures should also deepen the practitioners' understanding of developmental issues and varying learning styles of diverse students. Furthermore, individuals must put forth some effort to make connections with groups of people different from themselves. This may mean going to a church in a racially mixed community or volunteering to mentor a young person of color. For a detailed explanation of the student affairs core competencies and characteristics of a multiculturally competent student affairs practitioner, readers are directed to Pope and Reynolds (1997). The characteristics that practitioners should hone and embrace are noted in Table 6.2.

Table 6.2. Characteristics of a Multiculturally Competent Student Affairs Practitioner

Awareness	Knowledge	Skills
A belief that differences are valuable and that learning about others who are culturally different is necessary and rewarding	Knowledge of diverse cultures and oppressed groups (that is, history, traditions, values, customs, resources, issues)	Ability to identify and openly discuss cultural differences and issues
A willingness to take risks and see them as necessary and important for personal and professional growth	Information about how change occurs for individual values and behaviors	Ability to assess the impact of cultural differences on communication and effectively communicate across those differences
A personal commitment to justice, social change, and combating oppression	Knowledge about the ways that cultural differences affect verbal and nonverbal communication	Capability to empathize and genuinely connect with individuals who are different from themselves
A belief in the value and significance of their own cultural heritage and worldview as a starting place for understanding others who are culturally different from them	Knowledge about how gender, class, race and ethnicity, language, nationality, sexual orientation, age, religion or spirituality, disability, and ability affect individuals and their experiences	Ability to incorporate new learning and prior learning in new situations
A willingness to examine, and when necessary, challenge and change, their own values, worldview, assumptions, and biases	Information about culturally appropriate resources and how to make referrals	Ability to gain the trust and respect of individuals who are culturally different from themselves
An openness to change and belief that change is necessary and positive	Information about the nature of institutional oppression and power	Capability to accurately assess their own multicultural skills, comfort level, growth, and development

Table 6.2. Characteristics of a Multiculturally Competent Student Affairs Practitioner (cont'd)

Awareness	Knowledge	Skills
An acceptance of other worldviews and perspectives and a willingness to acknowledge that they, as individuals, do not have all the answers	Knowledge about identity development models and the acculturation process for members of oppressed groups and its impact on individuals, groups, intergroup relations, and society	Ability to differentiate individual differences, cultural differences, and universal similarities
A belief that cultural differences do not have to interfere with effective communication or meaningful relationships	Knowledge about group differences and understanding of multiple identities and multiple oppressions	Ability to challenge and support individuals and systems around oppression issues in a manner that optimizes multicultural interventions
Awareness of their own cultural heritage and how it affects their worldview, values, and assumptions	Information and understanding of internalized oppression and its impact on identity and self-esteem	Ability to make individual, group, and institutional multicultural interventions
Awareness of their own behavior and its impact on others	Knowledge about institutional barriers which limit access to and success in higher education for members of oppressed groups	Ability to use cultural knowledge and sensitivity to make more culturally sensitive and appropriate interventions
Awareness of the interpersonal process that occurs within a multicultural dyad	Knowledge about systems theories and how systems change	

Source: R. L. Pope and A. L. Reynolds, "Student Affairs Core Competencies: Integrating Multicultural Awareness, Knowledge, and Skills." *Journal of College Student Development,* 1997, *38*(3), 271.

What Works in Diversity Programming?

The national student affairs organizations should be leading the charge and modeling the way for diversity programming. The National Association for Student Personnel Administrators and the Association of American Colleges and Universities have collaborated and designed an institute called "Diversity: A Catalyst for Institutional Collaboration" (Greenstein, 1999). The group brings together faculty and administrators at various stages of diversity work to discuss how to create effective multicultural learning environments for all students. Overall, past participants have "deepened their understandings about the complexity of campus diversity and developed ways to move beyond one-shot programs to structurally infuse diversity into every fabric of their institutional lives" (Greenstein, 1999, p. 2).

Once a multiculturally competent student affairs administrator champions a clear mission and goal for diversity programming, a multiplicity of activities can be implemented for students, administrators, and faculty on large and small campuses. Creative programming has been implemented successfully at two-year and four-year institutions across the country. In regions that are not racially diverse, several small colleges clustered together can establish regional partnerships to provide diversity education to community members (Trompetter, 1999). For example, a Diversity Institute was established in northeastern Pennsylvania in 1993 at College Misericordia with the support of the presidents from University of Scranton, Kings College, Marywood University, and Wilkes University. The consortium is open to two-year and four-year colleges and universities, businesses, minority groups, and community residents, all of whom collaborate to consolidate their resources for diversity education. One outcome has been the implementation of a one-week diversity education camp to train high school students how to be culturally sensitive and caring citizens. Other small schools have designed and implemented programs with similar success. Mount St. Mary's College in Los Angeles has developed a Center for Intercultural Development that will provide curricular and cocurricular initiatives as well as research, recruitment, and retention efforts (Greenstein, 1999).

Students at Smith College launched an advertising campaign with signatures on a petition in support of diversity in higher education ("Smith College Students," 1999). The students wanted the community and the institution to know that their expanded knowledge about racial and ethnic issues and a multicultural campus would prepare them for a diverse world. The ad they placed in the local newspaper read: "As students at Smith College, we declare our support for maintaining and increasing diversity in college admissions. In our experience, policies that expand racial, ethnic, and socioeconomic diversity in higher education are essential in promoting equal access to education, improving the quality of education for all students, and contributing to equality of opportunity in the society at large" (p. 9).

The Religious and Spiritual Life Program at Wellesley College has students and faculty exploring different faiths such as Native African, Native American, Taoist, and Muslim, to name just a few ("Smith College Students," 1999). Workshops have enabled the participants to share spiritual and inspirational moments that have brought them closer together. Larger institutions may have diverse curriculums already prepared for their students; however, there are many other opportunities to have a culturally enriched environment for everyone.

Members of organizations such as fraternities and sororities were found to have lower scores on a measure of cultural sophistication than non-Greeks (Terenzini, Pascarella, and Blimling, 1996); thus, multicultural programming for these students is paramount. A method of getting the communication between cultures started is by getting members from African American and White Greek letter organizations together for cultural sensitivity activities (Howard-Hamilton, 1993). Using a variety of exercises to deconstruct myths and initiate conversations, the workshop could be an educational tool that leads to respect for the similarities and differences among the organizations. Obviously, students should be active participants in diversity programming. However, Dalton (1991) indicates "that students themselves can be highly effective educators and role models in efforts to reduce bias and promote an appreciation of differences" (p. 1).

In his book *Racism on Campus: Confronting Racial Bias Through Peer Interventions,* Dalton (1991) delineates methods for training students to be peer facilitators to confront campus bias. He stresses the importance of the peer culture on campus and how it can exert a tremendous amount of pressure on the behaviors of college students and influence their value system. Thus, the peer culture can be either an obstacle that thwarts the practitioner's and educator's efforts to create a diverse environment or a tool for eradicating bias and promoting tolerance and acceptance. An example of the peer intervention process is a racism reduction workshop in which students selected to be peer facilitators can process their own biases. The peer facilitators are also trained in conflict mediation and cultural awareness activities. After the training, the students are paired and become campus consultants or workshop leaders for organizations and classes wanting to learn about diversity issues. The peer teams could be comprised of a student of color and a white student to effectively model collaboration and understanding.

Exemplary multicultural affairs units can be found at Texas A&M University. The university has a Department of Multicultural Services within the Division of Student Affairs that provides the necessary funding and staff so the entire university can receive diversity education. Numerous cultural initiatives are available such as the five-day Diversity Institute, the University for Cultural Togetherness Program (U-ACT), Maximizing Opportunities for Staff to Achieve an Inclusive Campus Program (MOSAIC), and the Multicultural Student Leadership Forum (Department of Multicultural Services, n.d.). The university provides staff members to facilitate workshops and train students, staff, and faculty in diversity education.

The Dean of Students Office at the University of Florida has numerous cultural programs and activities throughout the academic year for the campus community. Two established cultural centers, the Institute of Black Culture (IBC) and La Casita, are located in prominent locations on campus. The two-story houses provide students with a cultural home and place to relax. Located at each site are computers, televisions with VCRs, meeting facilities, a library, and picnic area. The houses are supervised by a full-time coordinator and support staff. These houses are the central sites for annual activities such as African American History Month, Hispanic Heritage Month, Kwanzaa, and Three Kings, to name a few celebrations.

The IBC was also instrumental in bridging a cultural gap between African American and black students on campus (Howard-Hamilton, Ferguson, Rolle, and Alexander, 1997). Faculty, staff, and students were invited to a one-day off-campus cultural retreat to bring together students of color from the African Diaspora (African American, Caribbean, African, Black Latinos) to dialogue about issues that have typically impeded communications. The retreat led to the development of a new organization, Committee of Leaders Organizing Unification Relations. It is imperative that students of color find a way to collaborate, communicate, and connect with each other particularly on predominantly white campuses so that they will not feel alienated and marginalized. As students of color become more empowered to create new organizations and make important liaisons with other diverse groups, many majority students may feel threatened.

Many campuses are experiencing backlash to the diversity programming efforts on college campuses. Some individuals may find that speakers' views are offensive or that activities and programs are at the opposite end of the values continuum from their own.

Free Speech

Designing and implementing programs that promote a multicultural agenda may not be supported by the entire campus community. The dramatic increase in hate speech and harassment across the country is due, in part, to the significant strides made by students of color in affecting programs, curriculum, and admissions (Heumann and Church, 1997). Thus, students of color are part of a major dilemma because "as their assertiveness increases with their numbers, they are forced to deal with an increasing number of attacks" (Heumann and Church, 1977, p. 5).

The First Amendment to the U.S. Constitution protects the right of free speech and press so that people can peacefully assemble and petition the government if there are grievances. However, many students and campus organizations misinterpret the First Amendment by expressing their opinion at a time and place that is inappropriate or disregards the feelings of others (Paterson, 1998). If colleges and universities are to maintain some semblance of order during free speech activities (for example, controversial speakers or demonstrations), they must have clear and concise policies that allow open dialogue (Paterson, 1998). For example, forums can be one of three types: the limited public forum, the public forum, and the nonpublic forum. When there is an activity on campus, the institution can prepare for the effects of the program based upon the type of presentation that is made. If tickets are distributed for a speech to be held in a stadium or coliseum and demonstrators begin to disrupt the presentation, they may be asked to leave and escorted off the premises because they were guests invited to a limited public forum (Paterson, 1998). If, however, this presentation was made informally on the student parking lot, this is a public forum and the students may protest. The nonpublic forum—such as speech in classrooms and in some instances, residence halls—follows institutional guidelines and is not required to be open to the public.

It is important for students to hear divergent views and varying opinions. This free exchange of ideas is at the heart of the academic marketplace. In order to provide opportunities for individuals to demonstrate or speak freely on a multiplicity of issues, many campuses have open spaces that are designated (formally and informally) as free speech areas (Paterson, 1998). Another important issue is whether or not the First Amendment is an issue for private colleges. In most cases they are exempt because they are governed by their charter, license, or articles of incorporation (Barr, 1996). However, if a state law enforces the free speech doctrine, then the private institution must develop the appropriate guidelines (Paterson, 1998).

The issue of free speech can be addressed in a formal fashion by student affairs administrators who clearly believe in the right of all individuals to share their beliefs and values systems. This can be achieved by providing students, faculty, and administrators with guidelines that affirm free speech and delineate sanctions for violations of codes of conduct roused by bias or hate (Paterson, 1998). There can be a pall of political correctness that may chill discussion and limit learning if it is not handled in a way that promotes open dialogue. In other words, if students are not free to express unpopular and uninformed opinions, how can we challenge their beliefs regarding bigotry and recreate a new frame of reference or worldview? This question is handled in more detail in Howard-Hamilton, Phelps, and Torres (1998).

Conclusion

How will we treat the growing diverse populations on our college campuses? It is a difficult task to challenge old concepts and create new institutional structures. "It requires truly creative thinking about new structures, relationships, and partnerships" (Greenstein, 1999, p. 3). A plethora of multicultural programs at various institutions have been successful, and the scholars who play a key role in our national organizations have designed multicultural competencies that challenge practitioners, students, and faculty to learn more about diverse cultures. The new millennium has begun, and "our educational institutions were originally structured to affirm a population that is rapidly declining in its proportion of the whole" (Wilson, 1996, p. 6). As the demographic shifts occur on college campuses, as students of color are no longer being marginalized and are becoming part of the mainstream, a transformation must begin in and out of the classroom environments so that the students who leave our institutions will be multiculturally competent role models who advocate racial equality and inclusion.

References

American College Personnel Association and National Association for Student Personnel Administrators. *Principles of Good Practice for Student Affairs*. Washington, D.C.: American College Personnel Association, 1997.

Barr, M. J. "Legal Foundations of Student Affairs Practice." In S. R. Komives, D. B. Woodard Jr., and Associates (eds.), *Student Services: A Handbook for the Profession*. (3rd ed.) San Francisco: Jossey-Bass, 1996.

Dalton, J. C. "Racial and Ethnic Backlash in College Peer Culture." In J. C. Dalton (ed.), *Racism on Campus: Confronting Racial Bias Through Peer Interventions*. New Directions for Student Services, no. 56. San Francisco: Jossey-Bass, 1991.

Department of Multicultural Services. Texas Agriculture and Mechanical University. [http://aggieculture.tamu.edu/].

Greenstein, B. "Institutional Leadership and Commitment: Student and Academic Affairs Collaborate to Advance Campus Diversity." *Diversity Digest*. Washington, D.C.: Association of American Colleges and Universities, 1999. [http://www.inform.umd.edu/Digest/Sm99/collaborations.html]

Heumann, M., and Church, T. W. *Hate Speech on Campus: Cases, Case Studies, and Commentary*. Boston: Northeastern University Press, 1997.

Howard-Hamilton, M. F. "Greek Relationships in Black and White." *Journal of College Student Development*, 1993, *34*, 380–381.

Howard-Hamilton, M. F., Ferguson, A., Rolle, K., and Alexander, T. A. "Border Crossings: A 'Black' Cultural Retreat." *Journal of College Student Development*, 1997, *38*, 307–309.

Howard-Hamilton, M. F., Phelps, R. E., and Torres, V. "Meeting the Needs of All Students and Staff Members: The Challenge of Diversity." In D. L. Cooper and J. M. Lancaster (eds.), *Beyond Law and Policy: Reaffirming the Role of Student Affairs*. New Directions for Student Services, no. 82. San Francisco: Jossey-Bass, 1998.

Howard-Hamilton, M. F., Richardson, B. J., and Shuford, B. "Promoting Multicultural Education: A Holistic Approach." *College Student Affairs Journal*, 1998, *18*(1), 5–17.

King P. M., and Howard-Hamilton, M. F. "Becoming a Multiculturally Competent Student Affairs Professional." *Diversity on Campus: Reports from the Field*. Washington, D.C.: National Association of Student Personnel Administrators, 2000, 26–28.

King, P. M. "Improving Access and Educational Success for Diverse Students: Steady Progress but Enduring Problems." In C. S. Johnson and H. E. Cheatham (eds.), *Higher Education Trends for the Next Century: A Research Agenda for Student Success*. Washington, D.C.: American College Personnel Association, 1999.

McEwen, M. K., Roper, L. D., Bryant, D. R., and Langa, M. J. "Incorporating the Development of African American Students into Psychosocial Theories of Student Development." *Journal of College Student Development*, 1990, *31*, 429–436.

Paterson, B. G. "Expression, Harassment, and Hate Speech: Free Speech or Conduct Code Violation." In B. G. Patterson and W. L. Kibler (eds.), *The Administration of Campus Discipline: Student Organizational and Community Issues*. Asheville, N.C.: College Administration Publications, 1998.

Pope, R. L., and Reynolds, A. L. " Student Affairs Core Competencies: Integrating Multicultural Awareness, Knowledge, and Skills." *Journal of College Student Development*, 1997, *38*, 266–277.

"Smith College Students Launch Ad Campaign in Support of Diversity." *Diversity Digest*, Spring 1999, *3*(3), 9.

Stage, F. K., and Manning, K. (eds.) *Enhancing the Multicultural Campus Environment: A Cultural Brokering Approach*. New Directions for Student Services, no. 60. San Francisco: Jossey-Bass, 1992.

Terenzini, P. T., Pascarella, E. T., and Blimling, G. S. "Students' Out-of-Class Experiences and Their Influence on Learning and Cognitive Development: A Literature Review." *Journal of College Student Development*, 1996, *37*, 149–162.

Trompetter, L. "Regional Partnerships Help Schools Deepen Diversity Learning." *Diversity Digest*. Washington, D.C.: Association of American Colleges and Universities, 1999, *4*, 15.

Wilson, R. "Educating for Diversity." *About Campus,* 1996, *1*(2), 4–9, 30.

MARY HOWARD-HAMILTON *is associate professor and coordinator of the Student Personnel in Higher Education Program in the Department of Educational Leadership, Policy, and Foundations at the University of Florida, Gainesville.*

7

Too few date rape–prevention programs are designed specifically for men. This chapter presents a socialization-focused program and explores critical issues related to content development and selection, the delivery process, and evaluation strategies.

Programming for Men to Reduce Sexual Violence

Tracy Davis

Developing and presenting effective educational programs are key competencies for student development professionals. Among the most glaring deficits in educational programming for college students is effective rape prevention designed specifically for male audiences. This deficit is alarming due both to the severity of the consequences of rape for the victim and because "all-male audiences offer the greatest promise in truly reaching the potential of rape prevention" (Lonsway, 1996, p. 242).

This chapter is designed to assist college student affairs professionals obtain the information needed to plan, present, and assess rape prevention–educational programs for men. The first section will briefly discuss philosophical and other foundational issues. The problems and issues raised in this section should be considered both before and during the program development process. The second and third sections include a broad discussion regarding program content and process issues critical to effective rape prevention–educational efforts. The fourth section outlines challenges to evaluating rape prevention programs.

Philosophical Foundation

A significant problem in developing date rape–prevention programs is the lack of clarity regarding what causes men to rape. According to Ellis (1991) three distinct theories illuminate why men rape: feminist theory, evolutionary theory, and social learning theory. These theories illustrate that the phenomenon of rape is multidimensional and may be viewed from several perspectives. Feminist theory focuses on power relations between men and

women in social, political, and economic terms. Evolutionary theory empha-
sizes physiological sex differences, and social learning theory centers attention on the role of attitudes and imitative responses to peers, media and other
cultural cues. While feminist theory may accurately describe power differences and sex discrimination, designing programs for men emphasizing such
issues may serve to raise men's defensiveness, thereby inhibiting learning.
Likewise, evolutionary theory may accurately describe hormonal and bio-
logical dispositions toward aggression, but offers little hope in ethically mod-
ifying destructive behavior. Social learning theory, on the other hand, offers
the best explanation for date rape as opposed to other forms of rape
(Boeringer, Shehan and Akers, 1991; Davis, 1997). Since the overwhelming
percentage of rapes occurring on campus are date or acquaintance rapes,
social learning theory is a good foundation for guiding program development
for college men.

Social learning theory suggests that rape is primarily the function of
cultural influences that promote restrictive gender roles where coercive sexuality is accepted. This theory further proposes that individuals learn motives,
attitudes, and rationalizations that support sexually assaultive behavior. Sexual assault is, in other words, a learned behavior acquired through routine
social and environmental interaction. Rather than seeing date rape as representing a pathological disturbance in the perpetrator, social learning theory sees it as an extreme form of the traditionally socialized ways that men
and women act in the context of sexual relations. According to Berkowitz
(1994), for example, "it is the experience of masculinity itself—how men
think of themselves as men—that creates the psychological and cultural
environment that leads men to rape" (p. 7).

Although sex role socialization occurs over the span of a life, developmental tasks typically confronted by traditional-aged college men may also
be a key factor in men's use of sexual aggression. For example, the two most
fundamental emotions with which students grapple are "aggression and sex"
(Chickering, 1969, p. 11). In addition, establishing identity, including gender role identity, is a central task most college students must manage
(Chickering, 1969; Erickson, 1968). Moreover, the male college student
"typically pursues these developmental tasks within the confines of the traditional male role" (May, 1989, p. 12). Social learning, models of sex role
development, and student development theory together suggest that rape
prevention programs for men should include components that address the
messages about and mechanisms through which sex roles are taught and
reinforced.

Program Content

Program components should grow out of and be consistent with salient theories. This section briefly describes the content of a rape prevention program
for men that is focused on sex role socialization and was developed through

careful consideration of relevant theories. Program segments are guided not only by social learning theory but are also tailored for the intended audience using student development theory (for example, Chickering, 1969) and a model of men's gender identity development (O'Neil, 1981).

Key program objectives include helping participants explore their own attitudes and listen to others' opinions about sex roles and date rape; understand cultural forces that contribute to the acceptability of sexual aggression; deconstruct potentially harmful sex role socialization messages embedded in popular sitcoms; and identify distinctions between consensual and coercive sex. The introduction and key components of a model program focused on sex role socialization follows.

Program Introduction. Like most programs, the socialization-focused intervention begins with a brief introduction of the presenter and the program. The presenter should establish credibility, briefly state the purpose of the program, and establish rapport with the audience by acknowledging that some participants might feel resentment about attending a mandatory program. The presenter can also help avoid a preaching style by acknowledging his or her own sex-typed beliefs that have developed through socialization into this culture. A final component of the introduction should include the presenter reading some form of a safe environment contract that establishes permission to ask questions that may sound "stupid," acknowledges that we are all a product of a culture that makes it difficult to discuss issues about sex, and states that we have a responsibility to do something about it.

Sex Role Socialization Messages. Following the introduction, participants are asked to brainstorm a list of adjectives that describe both men and women in American culture. Once the facilitator has written all of the adjectives on newsprint, the group is asked to compare the lists. Inevitably, the lists contain responses at polar opposites (for example, emotional vs. unemotional). To illustrate how strongly these beliefs are held, the facilitator then asks about penalties for men and women who step outside of these stereotypic roles. The last discussion question in this component challenges participants to think about how these messages about sex-appropriate behavior are communicated (for example, advertising, television, movies, peers, parents, church).

Deconstructing the Messages. Participants then are asked to break up into small groups. Several popular sitcom clips, each illustrating an important connection between sex role socialization and rape, are presented. The groups are given the following instructions: "following each clip, your group's task is to discuss all of the possible ways people might respond to the questions raised. As a group you will then discuss how each member feels about the questions and whether you agree or not, and why. Try to answer the questions according to your first impulse, and then, after everyone has given his opinion, determine if there are any other perspectives." Sitcom clips that illustrate sex role differences, consent, or any of the four gender role conflict factors identified by O'Neil (1981) are appropriate. The four factors include (1) success, power, and competition; (2) restrictive emotionality; (3) restrictive affectionate behavior among men; and (4) conflicts between work and other relationships. For example, I have used a *Seinfeld* episode clip where the character Jerry Seinfeld is cajoling Elaine Benes to "give him another chance" to perform sexually so that she achieves orgasm. After the clip the following small group discussion questions are raised: Was Jerry really interested in his partner's satisfaction or his own performance? Do men feel pressure to "score"? What are some of the ways men place this kind of pressure on each other? What can we do to minimize this pressure? Another example, related to the issue of consent, is a *Friends* sitcom clip where early in the show the character Rachel clearly tells Ross that they will never have an intimate relationship; later in the show, Rachel walks up to Ross and kisses him. The following questions are raised in small group discussion: Do women say no when they really mean yes? How can a man tell if a woman means what she says? What should a man do if he feels he is getting mixed messages?

While these examples are somewhat outdated, plenty of contemporary sitcoms and movies illustrate sex role socialization messages related to date rape. Program developers can easily find usable messages in popular sitcoms, advertisements, music videos, movies, and magazines.

An optional strategy sometimes used to reinforce the idea that we are all affected by media, peers, and popular culture is to ask everyone who owns something with a Nike swoosh logo attached or wearing something that is being massively promoted in the media to stand. The Nike example can be particularly effective when connected to the slogan "just do it."

Addressing Consent. The final major component of this program is aimed at clarifying the parameters of sexual consent and the definition of rape. The presenter begins by posing the question, "A couple has sex. One doesn't ask and the other doesn't say no. Could this be rape?" After the small groups have discussed their responses, the facilitator leads a discussion aimed at clarifying that the existence of pressure, use of alcohol, or lack of clear communication reduces the likelihood that consensual sex has occurred. A legal definition of rape and sexual assault is handed out to reinforce the fact that the lack of consent may lead to criminal prosecution. Finally, Allgeier and Turner-Royster's (1991) model for obtaining consent is offered as a method for communicating about sexual relations. This model essentially challenges individuals to learn to negotiate a set of conditions under which sexual feelings may be acted upon. For example, participants are asked to consider the risks posed by previous relationships, contraceptives, the type of sex desired, and the meaning of any interaction.

While the components discussed in this section have been effectively used in rape prevention efforts with male audiences, they are not the only promising strategies currently being studied. Berkowitz (1994) also advocates the use of sex role socialization components in rape prevention work with men, but encourages the use of peer training programs. Other studies have found positive although mixed results using empathy induction strategies (Foubert and McEwen, 1998; Rosenthal, Heesacker, and Neimeyer, 1995; Schewe and O'Donohue, 1996). In addition, Heppner, Humphrey, Hillenbrand-Gunn, and DeBord (1995) have successfully employed an interactive drama program that appeared to effectively stimulate learning.

Program Process Issues

While program content areas must be constructed thoughtfully and guided by theory, the success of any didactic intervention often depends on the process by which the program is implemented. Program process issues are aimed at making the content palatable to the learner, effectively engaging the learner, reducing defensiveness, and facilitating thoughtful evaluation of the information being presented. That is, process strategies should be geared toward enhancing the "learnability" of the intended outcomes. Since student development programs often cover content areas that are controversial and easily raise defenses among participants, it is important that program developers meet this challenge directly and use facilitative styles and strategies that will promote learning.

Central Route Versus Peripheral Route Processing. One theoretical model that can help program developers consider how to engage participants effectively in the learning process and change attitudes is Petty and Cacioppo's (1986) elaboration likelihood model (ELM). This model suggests that when program participants are motivated to process information and the presented material is perceived as personally relevant, there is greater likelihood that central route attitude change will occur. Conversely, participants who lack motivation to hear a message or who believe the message is not valuable are more likely to attend to peripheral cues rather than the program content. Central route processing, according to Petty and Cacioppo, tends to produce greater attitude change, predicts later behavior more strongly, and leads to more resistance toward counterarguments in subsequent presentations.

Two recent studies used the ELM to design their programs and found that an all-male audience (Gilbert, Heesacker, and Gannon, 1991) and an interactive drama (Heppner, Humphrey, Hillenbrand-Gunn, and DeBord, 1995) effectively promoted participants' central route processing. These results suggest that programmers should focus not only on the content of the interventions but also the learning strategies employed. Using short video stimulus and engaging participants in interactive discussion are processes aimed at making the material presented relevant and increasing participants' motivation.

Sitcoms and Socialization as Process Issues. Popular sitcom clips are also used because viewing television is one of the activities through which sex role stereotypes and attitudes are initially learned (Klumas and Marchant, 1994). The sitcoms, therefore, serve three purposes. First, use of the clips engages participants and reduces defensiveness, thus preparing them for the learning messages. Second, the follow-up questions challenge audience members to take responsibility for deconstructing and thinking critically about the underlying sex role messages and their connection to sexual assault. Third, by using this common socialization medium, participants gain firsthand experience in becoming critical consumers of potentially dysfunctional messages.

This strategy can be traced back to the theories discussed earlier. The program uses some of the same processes by which social learning theory suggests individuals learn attitudes supportive of rape. In addition, participants are encouraged to begin taking responsibility to develop their own sex role identity rather than uncritically absorbing messages promoted by media, peers, and other "masters of the universe." Ideally, the strategies promote central route processing, encourage participants to think deeply about a socialization pattern that may be conducive to date rape, and help them interrupt messages that may influence rape-supportive attitudes.

Constructing a Safe Learning Environment. Since discussing messages about sexuality and sex role socialization is somewhat taboo, it is important that the environment is psychologically safe and conducive to meaningful sharing of personal beliefs. One strategy that has been widely discussed and consistently supported in the sexual assault prevention literature is to present programs to all-male audiences (Berkowitz, 1994; Foubert and Marriott, 1997; Schewe and O'Donohue, 1993). Men are generally more willing to discuss sexual assault issues honestly without women in the room. This may be particularly true for men initially struggling with sex role identity issues. Research has consistently demonstrated more effective programmatic results when presentations are made to all-male audiences compared to mixed audiences (Earle, 1996; Kline, 1993; Prince, 1994).

Attributes of the facilitator may also impact the safety and effectiveness of the program. Presenters should feel comfortable discussing sex and have the ability to sensitively challenge audience members who may be hostile or defensive. Members of the audience must feel comfortable expressing conflicting values and ideas. In addition to the facilitator's style, several authors have suggested that male peer-educators may be the most effective individuals in changing rape-supportive attitudes (Berkowitz, 1994; Earle, 1996; Foubert and Marriott, 1997). Peer-educators have several advantages in presenting the sex role socialization–focused program. First, audience members more likely will identify with a peer and believe that a peer will understand them. Second, like the use of sitcoms, using peer-presenters uses a vehicle (peers) through which sex role messages are often learned.

Finally, another important strategy for creating a safe learning environment is to break large audiences into small interactive discussion groups. This strategy helps create the kind of intimacy necessary to discuss sensitive and potentially embarrassing topics. Moreover, the facilitator has a better chance of engaging participants in the learning process and meeting members where they are by asking interesting questions that require safer, small group involvement.

Challenges in Evaluation and Method

Programs similar to the one discussed in this chapter have been found to decrease rape-myth acceptance (Gilbert, Heesacker, and Gannon, 1991; Rosenthal, Heesacker, and Neimeyer, 1995) and reduce other rape-supportive beliefs (Earle, 1996; Frazier, Valtinson, and Candell, 1994; Schewe and O'Donohue, 1996). Although these results might suggest that programming efforts have been highly effective, such a conclusion remains elusive. Most programs are not evaluated systematically in a manner that allows much confidence in the results. This section focuses on the significant challenges to assessing the effectiveness of rape prevention programs for men.

Population Issues. Rape prevention programmers often lament their inability to get those most in need of an educational intervention to attend. One strategy for programmers to use in order to help avoid "preaching to the converted" is to access high-risk subcultures—such as fraternities, athletic teams, and other all-male environments. Studies have found consistently that membership in a fraternity is associated with higher levels of participation in sexual coercion (Boeringer, 1996; Frinter and Rubinson, 1993; Worth, Matthews, and Coleman, 1990). Studies also support the higher representation of male college athletes in reports of battering and sexual assault (Crosset, Ptacek, McDonald, and Benedict, 1996; Koss and Gaines, 1993). Gaining access to these subcultures often will require the help of insiders as well as patience in establishing the kind of trust necessary to develop a long-term relationship. A significant advantage of working with Greek chapters and athletic teams is that all members, not just those who would normally attend such an educational program, often can be required to attend by a coach or chapter president.

Another strategy aimed at helping assess the effectiveness of a program for those most in need of an intervention is to measure the risk level of participants. Since we do not have direct measures of rape proclivity, investigators can use such measures associated with rape proclivity as Burt's (1980) Adversarial Sexual Beliefs Scales or Malamuth's (1981) Likelihood of Raping Scale. Including measures secondarily associated with rape proclivity may help us discover which programs work best for those at higher risk for perpetrating sexual assault.

Multiple Assessment Methods. Most rape prevention programs use measures of intervention effectiveness that are related only to a single attitude (for example, rape-myth acceptance). While this strategy may elicit some important data, there are other creative methods to acquire outcome information. Heppner, Humphrey, Hillenbrand-Gunn, and DeBord (1995), for example, used phone calls to participants four months following their intervention asking if they would be willing to volunteer to help with rape prevention activities and willing to support a fee increase for prevention programs on campus.

A less direct method of assessing participants' behavioral intentions would be to include the Likelihood to Rape (Malamuth, 1981) or Likelihood to Use Force (Briere and Malamuth, 1983) scales. The former scale asks participants to respond to the question "If you could be assured of not being caught or punished, how likely would you be to rape?" Responses range from one, not at all likely, to five, very likely. Berg, Lonsway, and Fitzgerald (1999) suggested modifications to the Likelihood to Rape scale that focus on intended behaviors. These behavior-related strategies can give some information about participants beyond the typical attitude measures.

Participant knowledge can be assessed with the Comprehension of Consent/Coercion Measure (CCC), developed by Gibson and Humphrey (1993). The CCC is designed to measure a person's ability to recognize the difference between coerced and consensual sex. Participants read two short vignettes describing a typical date that involves sexual activity and respond to questions which ask them to decide whether the activity occurred after consent or coercion.

Assessment methods and instruments should be matched according to the program educational components. The CCC, for example, would be a good measure for the socialization-focused intervention because there is a consent-related educational segment. The tactic of using behavior-related and knowledge assessment tools is, furthermore, especially important because attitude change has been shown to be very unstable. Researchers who use only an initial posttest may falsely presume that attitudes have changed when in fact a follow-up posttest weeks or months later might yield quite different results.

Follow-Up Posttesting. Many studies indicate that positive attitude changes measured immediately following a program tend to rebound to pre-intervention levels in follow-up posttests (Davis, 1997; Frazier, Valtinson, and Candell, 1994; Heppner, Humphrey, Hillenbrand-Gunn, and DeBord, 1995; Prince, 1994). In fact, the evidence strongly suggests that studies that use only an initial posttest of participant attitudes face serious threats to the validity of their results. One possible explanation for an initial decline and later rebound in rape-supportive attitudes is that pretesting, administered immediately prior to the program, sensitizes participants to the measure. Moreover, testing effects have been found in studies of rape prevention–program investigations that compared posttest scores of comparable groups who either did or did not receive pretesting (Harrison, Downes, and Williams, 1991; Lenihan, Rawlins, Eberly, Buckley, and others, 1992).

Another explanation for attitude rebound may be that learning and attitude change do not progress in a linear fashion. It is possible, for example, that follow-up posttests that appear to indicate a reversal of positive changes may actually indicate a temporary state prior to more permanent integration of new knowledge or awareness. Longitudinal studies could begin to address this question. For now, those investigating the effectiveness of rape prevention programs must rely on multiple assessment methods and more than one follow-up posttest period.

Other Challenges to Rape Prevention Program Evaluation. Challenges associated with careful rape prevention program evaluation are similar to Paul's (1967) recognition of the problems associated with counseling research. He suggested that in order to deal with the overwhelming complexity and number of confounding variables associated with counseling investigations, researchers should examine the question "What treatment, by whom, is most effective for this individual with that specific problem, and under which set of circumstances?" (p. 111). What is needed, then, are carefully controlled studies that use tailored treatments presented by trained professionals to high-risk individuals, within specified contexts.

Summary

Student affairs professionals must be intentional in constructing educational programs grounded in theory. Social learning theory provides the best framework for understanding date rape and developing programmatic interventions for men on college campuses. Using theory to shape the content of our interventions is, however, insufficient for developing an effective program aimed at preventing men's perpetration of sexual assault. Critical process and delivery issues must be thoughtfully implemented in order to reduce men's defensiveness and create an environment conducive to learning. Interactive programs designed for all-male audiences and delivered by male peers are minimum requirements for working with college men on the issue of rape prevention. Finally, if we are to accurately assess the effectiveness of our rape prevention programs, we would be well advised to consider the methodological challenges that most previous studies have failed to adequately address.

References

Allgeier, E. R., and Turner-Royster, B. J. "New Approaches to Dating and Sexuality." In E. Gauerholz and M. Koralewski (eds.), *Sexual Coercion: A Source Book on Its Nature, Causes, and Prevention.* Lexington, Mass.: Lexington Books, 1991.

Berg, D. R., Lonsway, K. A., and Fitzgerald, L. F. "Rape Prevention Education for Men: The Effectiveness of Empathy-Induction Techniques." *Journal of College Student Development,* 1999, *40*, 219–234.

Berkowitz, A. D. (ed.). *Men and Rape: Theory, Research, and Prevention Programs in Higher Education.* San Francisco: Jossey-Bass, 1994.

Boeringer, S. B. "Influences of Fraternity Membership, Athletics, and Male Living Arrangements on Sexual Aggression." *Violence Against Women,* 1996, *2,* 134–147.

Boeringer, S. B., Shehan, C. L., and Akers, R. L. "Social Learning in Sexual Coercion and Aggression: Assessing the Contribution of Fraternity Membership." *Family Relations,* 1991, *40*, 58–64.

Briere, J., and Malamuth, N. M. "Self-Reported Likelihood of Sexually Aggressive Behavior: Attitudinal Versus Sexual Explanations." *Journal of Research Personality*, 1983, *17*, 315–323.

Burt, M. "Cultural Myths and Supports for Rape." *Journal of Personality and Social Psychology*, 1980, *38*, 217–230.

Chickering, A. W. *Education and Identity*. San Francisco: Jossey-Bass, 1969.

Crosset, T. W., Ptacek, J., McDonald, M. A., and Benedict, J. R. "Male Student Athletes and Violence Against Women." *Violence Against Women*, 1996, *2*, 163–179.

Davis, T. L. "The Effectiveness of a Sex Role Socialization-Focused Date Rape Prevention Program in Reducing Rape-Supportive Attitudes in College Fraternity Men." Unpublished doctoral dissertation, Department of Counseling, Rehabilitation, and Student Development, University of Iowa, 1997.

Earle, J. P. "Acquaintance Rape Workshops: Their Effectiveness in Changing the Attitudes of First-Year College Men." *NASPA Journal*, 1996, *34*, 2–18.

Ellis, L. "A Synthesized (Biosocial) Theory of Rape." *Journal of Consulting and Clinical Psychology*, 1991, *39*, 631–642.

Erickson, E. H. *Identity: Youth and Crisis*. New York: W. W. Norton, 1968.

Foubert, J. D., and Marriott, K. A. "Effects of a Sexual Assault Prevention Program on Men's Belief in Rape Myths." *Sex Roles*, 1997, *36*, 257–266.

Foubert, J. D., and McEwen, M. "An All-Male Rape Prevention Peer Education Program: Decreasing Fraternity Men's Behavioral Intent to Rape." *Journal of College Student Development*, 1998, *39*, 548–556.

Frazier, P., Valtinson, G., and Candell, S. "Evaluation of a Coeducational Interactive Rape Prevention Program." *Journal of Counseling and Development*, 1994, *73*, 153–158.

Frinter, M. P., and Rubinson, L. "Acquaintance Rape: The Influence of Alcohol, Fraternity Membership, and Sports Team Membership." *Journal of Sex Education and Therapy*, 1993, *19*, 272–284.

Gibson, D. B., and Humphrey, C. F. "Educating in Regards to Sexual Violence: An Interactional Dramatic Acquaintance Rape Intervention." Unpublished manuscript, Sexual Violence Program, University of Minnesota, 1993.

Gilbert, B. J., Heesacker, M., and Gannon, L. J. "Changing the Sexual Aggression-Supportive Attitudes of Men: A Psychoeducational Intervention." *Journal of Counseling Psychology*, 1991, *38*, 197–203.

Harrison, P. J., Downes, J., and Williams, M. D. "Date and Acquaintance Rape: Perceptions and Attitude Change Strategies." *Journal of College Student Development*, 1991, *32*, 131–139.

Heppner, M. J., Humphrey, C. F., Hillenbrand-Gunn, T. L., and DeBord, K. A. "The Differential Effects of Rape Prevention Programming on Attitudes, Behavior, and Knowledge." *Journal of Counseling Psychology*, 1995, *42*, 508–518.

Kline, R. J. "The Effects of a Structured-Group Rape-Prevention Program on Selected Male Personality Correlates of Abuse Toward Women." Unpublished doctoral dissertation, Lehigh University, 1993.

Klumas, A. L., and Marchant, T. "Images of Men in Popular Sitcoms." *Journal of Men's Studies*, 1994, *2*, 269–285.

Koss, M., and Gaines, J. "The Prediction of Sexual Aggression by Alcohol Use, Athletic Participation and Fraternity Affiliation." *Journal of Interpersonal Violence*, 1993, *8*, 94–108.

Lenihan, G. O., Rawlins, M. E., Eberly, C. G., Buckley, B., and others. "Gender Differences in Rape Supportive Attitudes Before and After a Date Rape Education Intervention." *Journal of College Student Development*, 1992, *33*, 331–338.

Lonsway, K. A. "Preventing Acquaintance Rape Through Education: What Do We Know?" *Psychology of Women Quarterly*, 1996, *20*, 229–265.

Malamuth, N. M. "Rape Proclivity Among Males." *Journal of Social Issues*, 1981, *20*, 138–157.

May, R. J. "The Developmental Journey of the Male College Student." *Men's Studies Review,* 1989, *6,* 10–16.

O'Neil, J. M. "Patterns of Gender-Role Conflict and Strain: The Fear of Femininity in Men's Lives." *Personnel and Guidance Journal,* 1981, *60,* 203–210.

Paul, G. L. "Strategy of Outcome Research in Psychotherapy." *Journal of Consulting Psychology,* 1967, *31,* 109–118.

Petty, R. E., and Cacioppo, J. T. *Communication and Persuasion: Central and Peripheral Routes to Attitude Change.* New York: Springer-Verlag, 1986.

Prince, E. D. "Male Attitudes Toward Acquaintance Sexual Assault: Comparison of Single-Gender Versus Mixed-Gender Group Educational Intervention." Unpublished doctoral dissertation, University of Oregon, 1994.

Rosenthal, E. H., Heesacker, M., and Neimeyer, G. J. "Changing the Rape-Supportive Attitudes of Traditional and Non-Traditional Males and Females." *Journal of Counseling Psychology,* 1995, *42,* 171–177.

Schewe, P., and O'Donohue, W. "Rape Prevention with High Risk Males: Short-Term Outcome of Two Interventions." *Archives of Sexual Behavior,* 1996, *25,* 455–471.

Schewe, P., and O'Donohue, W. "Rape Prevention: Methodological Problems and New Directions." *Clinical Psychology Review,* 1993, *13,* 667–682.

Worth, D. M., Matthews, P. A., and Coleman, W. R. "Sex Role, Group Affiliation, Family Background, and Courtship Violence in College Students." *Journal of College Student Development,* 1990, *31,* 250–254.

TRACY DAVIS is assistant professor of counselor education and college student personnel at Western Illinois University. His dissertation, on which this chapter is based, won the 1999 Dissertation of the Year award from both the American College Personnel Association and the National Association of Student Personnel Administrators.

8

*This chapter offers examples of proven practices in pro-
gramming and highlights programs in service learning,
alcohol awareness, leadership, diversity education, and
community building.*

Promising Practices in Programming:
An Annotated List of Model Programs

Heather O'Neill

The program descriptions contained in this chapter are intended to provide
concrete examples of promising practices in programming. The programs
chosen for inclusion have clear goals, measurable learning outcomes for
both the students who participate and the students who administer them,
and were evaluated accordingly. The description of each program includes,
when possible, a statement of the program's purpose and contact information for the sponsoring individual or institution. The programs are divided
into five categories: service learning, leadership, community building, alcohol awareness, and diversity.

Service Learning

Programs focused on learning through volunteer community services are
explored next.

Active Learners Involved via Experience (ALIVE). ALIVE is a series
of three programs targeted primarily at first- and second-year students who
may not realize the range of opportunities available to them on their college
campus. The focus is on experiential education or learning by doing, as well
as on the idea that learning can occur outside the classroom. Students are
encouraged to attend and participate actively in each of the three sessions.
At each individual program, the other two sessions are discussed to allow
students to build on previous experiences and remind them of upcoming
opportunities. Each program is held in the same place, at the same time,
every two weeks to uphold the continuity of the series. Contact: Donna
Denoncourt, Assistant Director, #9665 Hinman College, Binghamton University, Binghamton, N.Y. 13902-6009. Telephone: (607) 777-4716.

NEW DIRECTIONS FOR STUDENT SERVICES, no. 90, Summer 2000   © Jossey-Bass Publishers

Labor of Love. Labor of Love is a program designed to facilitate the participation of incoming students, residential living leaders, faculty, and staff in volunteer projects during the first days of the fall semester. Through the program, university community members provide a valuable service to the local community and incoming students begin to develop ties to their new home away from home. Contact: Tom Richardson, Lower Level Delzell Hall, 910 Fremont Street, University of Wisconsin-Stevens Point, Stevens Point, Wis. 54481. Telephone: (715) 346-3511.

Scholarships and Service. All students who receive institutional financial aid in the form of scholarships or grants at Mount Olive College are required to provide twenty hours of community service each semester. Students may perform this service either on or off campus and must keep a record of their volunteer hours in order to remain eligible for scholarships and grants. The Board of Trustees instituted this program and believes that it is supportive of the college's mission and a unique way to encourage service. Contact: Karen Van Norman, Student Development, Mount Olive College, 634 Henderson Street, Mount Olive, N.C. 28365. Telephone: (919) 658-7167. E-mail: (kvannorman@exhange.moc.edu).

EMPOWER. EMPOWER is a fourteen-week leadership program designed for approximately twenty-five students who are interested in learning about social inequalities and exploring the relationship between leadership and social justice. This program seeks to introduce participants to a variety of social issues, as well as to highlight professionals who model the idea of the citizen leader by dedicating their lives and careers to serving their community. Student mentors and participants in the program work within teams to develop and participate in a service learning project while simultaneously engaging in interdisciplinary research on their respective social justice issue. The EMPOWER curriculum exposes students to interdependent, nonhierarchical forms of leadership and provides them with opportunities to develop or augment their leadership skills. Each small group develops its own principles of unity that members draw upon to maintain the integrity of the team throughout the program.

Through an interactive workshop, students are challenged to examine the similarities, differences, and connections between charity, community service, activism, and service learning. Subsequent to their service experiences, student mentors lead each group of participants in various reflection activities that are intended to broaden their preconceived notions of service to include activism and social change. The EMPOWER curriculum was designed specifically with both the mission of the university and the mission of the student affairs division in mind. The issues with which students grapple during the course challenge them to reflect upon their values, think critically about social justice issues, connect their academic and personal knowledge with their service experience, and ultimately become more informed and action-oriented citizens who have the skills and ability to make substantive contributions to their communities. In order to support students in these challenging endeavors, facilitators use teaching and group facilitation methods that accommodate and validate diverse perspectives, personalities, and learning styles. Contact: Elizabeth O'Reggio-Wilson, Director, Student Leadership and Service Learning, 111 Warfield Hall, Miami University, Oxford, Ohio 45056. Telephone: (513) 529-2961. E-mail: (oreggie@muohio.edu).

EXCEL. The EXCEL program encourages and enables students to participate in a wide variety of activities, clubs, leadership programs, and campus or community arts experiences, and to document their service and awards. During the two to four years that students are on campus, they build a student development transcript to accompany their academic transcript. The goal of the program is to offer students a diverse college experience, assist with their employment or graduate school search, and help them grow as global citizens. Contact: Jeanne Takeda, Director of Student Development, Northwood University—Florida Campus, 2600 North Military Trail, West Palm Beach, Fla. 33409. Telephone: (561)478-5558. E-mail: (takeda@northwood.edu).

PreSERVE. The PreSERVE program is a pre-orientation service experience for incoming students at Elon College. These students spend a week prior to the start of the fall semester working with Habitat for Humanity. The goal of the program is to provide a means to connect students to the campus and community in a meaningful way from the start of their college careers. Contact: Tait Arend, Kernodle Center for Service Learning, 2999 Campus Box, Elon College, Elon College, N.C. 27244. Telephone: (910) 584-2102. E-mail: (arendt@numen.elon.edu).

Leadership

Several programs that highlight leadership development appear here.

Leadership Development Series. The Leadership Development Series consists of a sequence of workshops on topics of interest to students who wish to become more creative, effective, and productive leaders. Topics include mediation, gender communication, goal setting, values, leading with integrity, assertive communication, working with diverse populations, and leadership and spirituality. Contact: Janey Musgrave, Director, Center for Student Leadership, Ethics, and Public Service, Box 7306, North Carolina State University, Raleigh, N.C. 27695-7306. Telephone: (919) 515-9248. E-mail: (janey_musgrave@ncsu.edu). Web site (http://www.fis.ncsu.edu/slc/).

Student Leader Fellowship Program. The Student Leader Fellowship Program is committed to developing competent, ethical, and community-centered leaders. Over a two-year period, students participate in six component areas focusing on self-development and community involvement. These components are a fall retreat, a mentor program to match participating students with a community leader, a semester-long course on Leadership Theory and Practice, Skill Builders Leadership Workshops, a community service internship, and special opportunities for student fellows to meet notable leaders and university guests. Contact: Rachel Harris, Student Leader Fellowship Program, 1206 Don H. Bottum University Center, Northern Michigan University, 1401 Presque Isle Avenue, Marquette, Mich. 49855-5370. Telephone: (906) 227-1771. E-mail: (raharris@nmu.edu). Web site: (http://www.nmu.edu/salp/slfp.htm).

Leadership House. The purpose of the Leadership House is to bring students together in a living environment that grounds them in a shared experience and empowers them to serve and lead, as well as grapple with the ideals of servant-leadership as it pertains to their lives in an experiential setting. The program encourages students to take a shared responsibility for building a community of learners and to model the ethical uses of power, acceptance, and empathy for others. Participating students also learn the value of foresight and intuition and can develop their powers of persuasion, rather than impose their will on others. Contact: Frank Hamilton, University of South Florida, 4202 Fowler Avenue, BSN 3528, Tampa, Fla. 33620. Telephone: (813) 974-4945. E-mail: (fhamilto@coba.usf.edu).

LeaderShape Miami. After two years of attending national LeaderShape conferences, Miami University students requested that their university extend participation in such opportunities to a wider range of students. To meet this need, Miami University now sponsors two annual LeaderShape Miami Institutes solely for Miami students. Each session of the Institute consists of a six-day program of interactive learning and provides the tools for students to learn to work in high-performing teams, practice decision making for ethical dilemmas, produce extraordinary results, learn to deal with change, clarify personal values and standards, and understand and respect the values of other individuals. Numerous faculty, staff, and alumni participate in the program as Cluster Facilitators who live with the participants for the entire six days, then return to campus to support the continued development and work of the student participants. The interaction of the students who have attended the institutes has transformed campus student organizations that had rarely worked together into organizations that value cooperation and collaboration. Contact: Dennis C. Roberts, Assistant Vice President of Student Affairs, 111 Warfield Hall, Miami University, Oxford, Ohio 45056. Telephone: (513) 529-2961. E-mail: (robertd2@muohio.edu).

Programming Board Self-Assessment. The Programming Board Self-Assessment is used by the University of North Carolina–Charlotte as a way for students to measure their growth and development after a year or more of serving on the campus programming board. Students complete the form prior to beginning their work with the board and again after working with the board for at least a year. The self-assessment consists of several Likert scales for students to rate their skills in areas such as problem solving, time management, flexibility, follow-through, and planning, as well as two programming scenarios for which students must develop action plans and identify potential obstacles. After completing the assessment, the students discuss their results and reflect on their experiences with the programming board advisor. The goal of the self-assessment is to help students articulate the skills and experience they gain by working on a programming board, as well as demonstrate the intentionality of the process of gaining those skills. Contact: Shane Windmeyer, Assistant Director of Student Activities, University of North Carolina–Charlotte. Telephone: (704) 547-2494. E-mail: (slwindme@email.uncc.edu).

Peer Consultants. The Peer Consultant Team is comprised of student leaders committed to the development of student organizations. The primary task of the peer consultants is to serve as resource persons to all student organizations, executive boards, and advisers on campus. Peer consultants accomplish this task by providing programs on leadership topics such as motivation, running effective meetings, and peer relations. In addition, the peer consultants offer opportunities for personal, organizational, or leadership development through campus-wide programming, workshops, and conferences. Students who are selected as peer consultants enroll in a semester-long course to help them develop the skills, knowledge, and experience necessary to work with student organizations. Contact: Dana L. Filchner, Leadership Program Coordinator, 205 Heth Student Center, Radford University, Radford, Va. 24142. Telephone: (540) 831-5255. E-mail: (dlfilchn@runet.edu).

Community Building

A sense of community is important to students. Promising programs with this objective appear here.

Common Reading Experience. Sponsored by the Office of Multicultural Affairs, the Common Reading Experience is an annual program for incoming students. Each spring, faculty and staff members select a book to be read by all incoming students, faculty, and staff members, and discussed in groups at the beginning of the fall semester. The goal of the Common Reading Experience is to provide the campus community with a universal reference point to encourage and facilitate communication. Contact: James Diedrick, Professor of English, 611 East Porter Street, Albion College, Albion, Mich. 49224. Telephone: (517) 629-0273. E-mail: (jdiedrick@alpha.albion.edu).

Mind, Body, and Soul. The Mind, Body, and Soul program is a finals-week stress reliever and opportunity to build community among students sharing a residence hall floor. The program consists of four stations through which the participants cycle. First, the student sits down in a quiet corner with a resident assistant and has an opportunity to talk about his or her feelings concerning exam week, vent his or her frustrations, and learn about ways to relieve stress. Next the student receives a shoulder massage from another resident assistant, then a hand massage from another resident assistant, and finally a back and neck massage from a professional masseuse. Contact: Dan Oltersdorf, Colorado State University. E-mail: (dano@peakpeak.com). Web site: (http://www.residentassistant.com).

Breakfast Club. The resident assistant staff at a new residence facility at Lehigh University created this program in order to establish traditions for the students assigned to the hall. Beginning on the first Sunday of the fall semester, the residence hall staff prepares and serves breakfast for the residents each Sunday. To promote the program, staff members distribute individual doorhangers in the shape of different breakfast foods for each program to remind students. Contact: Jennifer Hapgood, Residence Director, 48 Butler Court, Keene State College, Keene, N.H. 03431. Telephone: (603) 358-8996.

First Year Experience. The First Year Experience program provides a challenging and stimulating forum to make the transition to college easier for incoming students. The program encourages community building while confronting issues such as racism and sexism, which have the potential to diminish an atmosphere of care and trust. Each new student is assigned to a First Year Experience group with approximately fifteen students per group. Two student mentors who are upperclassmen and one faculty or staff facilitator periodically meet with their group of students during the first five weeks of the fall semester. The first group meeting is scheduled during the kickoff of the Week of Welcome for incoming students. The group sessions consist of intense discussion and reflection on personal experiences during which members build strong relationships with other group members and make the transition to the campus community. Suggested topics for the various sessions include family and differences, safety, spirituality, values, and personal integrity. Contact: Tamie Klumpyan, Director of Student Involvement and Campus Activities, Department of Leadership, Service, and Involvement, 100 Grant Street, St. Norbert College, DePere, Wis. 54115. Telephone: (920) 403-4023. E-mail: (KLUMTJ@ mail.snc.edu).

Senior Success Seminars. The Senior Success Seminar series targets the needs of graduating seniors, needs not typically addressed in the academic curriculum. The seminars are interactive educational programs designed to provide graduating seniors with practical information and skills for their lives after college. Seminar topics have included "Backpack to Briefcase: Understanding the Workplace Culture," "No Homework, Now What?: Leading a Balanced Life After Graduation," and "Transition to Graduate School." The Senior Launch Committee, the Office of Greek Affairs, and the Office of Alumni and Parent Programs sponsor the series. Contact: Lupita Temiquel, Assistant Director of Greek Affairs, 356 Shriver Center, Miami University, Oxford, Ohio 45056. Telephone: (513) 529-1462. E-mail: (Temiqugc@muohio.edu).

Alcohol Awareness

This section highlights some promising programs targeted to change student behaviors and attitudes about alcohol.

The Drinking Game. The purpose of the Drinking Game program is to provide an interactive format for students to learn about the dangers of binge drinking. The facilitator, with the assistance of an alcohol awareness counselor, compiles a list of questions on the topic of drinking and divides them into four categories: true or false, multiple choice, media, and fill in the blank. The participants are divided into teams that take turns moving around a game board and answering questions that correspond to the colored space on which they land. Sample questions and answers include: (1) True or false—one beer has the same number of calories as a hotdog. True. (2) Two times the percentage of alcohol content in a drink is called what? Proof. Following the game, the facilitator asks the participants how they felt about the game, what information surprised them, and what new information they gathered. Contact: Erin Thomas, Resident Assistant, University of Southern Maine. E-mail: Erin Thomas (ethoma71@mail.caps.maine.edu) or Dan Oltersdorf (dano@peakpeak.com). Web site: (http:// www. residentassistant.com).

National Collegiate Alcohol Awareness Week. In the past, the University of Delaware relied on individual departments and organizations to address alcohol use and abuse on a small scale. After being identified as an institution with a high rate of binge drinking, the university planned and coordinated campus-wide programming efforts for National Collegiate Alcohol Awareness Week. The university's goal is to raise awareness of this health issue affecting students and to change the campus culture with respect to binge drinking. Contact: Holli Harvey, Complex Coordinator, Gilbert/Harrington, 405 Academy Street, University of Delaware, Newark, Del. 19716. Telephone: (302) 831-2023.

Social Norms Approach. A new approach to alcohol prevention has resulted in reductions in binge drinking at several college campuses. The social norms approach assumes that much of behavior is influenced by how other members of social groups behave, and that beliefs about what others do, in this case their drinking, are often overestimated. Media campaigns to inform students of the accurate, more healthy norm have been used on a number of campuses with subsequent reductions in binge drinking of over 20 percent during a two-year period. These campaigns are designed to correct student misperceptions about alcohol consumption and help develop healthier social norms. The campuses involved include Northern Illinois University, the University of Arizona, Western Washington University, and Hobart and William Smith Colleges. On each of these campuses, media messages were developed with student involvement to provide information about the true, healthy norm. For example, at the University of Arizona, a series of posters and advertisements in the campus newspaper indicated that "Most U of A Students Have 4 or Fewer Drinks When They Party." The University of Arizona and other campuses have achieved significant reductions in binge drinking rates following such media campaigns.

Social norms media campaigns require careful documentation of actual and perceived patterns of drinking, education of campus leaders and "stakeholders," and development of media that has student appeal. Although intuitively simple, the approach requires careful planning and implementation for success (Berkowitz, 1998; Haines, 1998; Perkins, 1997).

Contact: Alan D. Berkowitz, Ph.D., Independent Consultant, 8031 Searsburg Road, Trumansburg, N.Y. 14886. Telephone: (607) 387-3789. Fax: (607) 387-9615. Web sites: Hobart and William Smith Colleges, (http://www.hws.edu/~alcohol); Northern Illinois University, (http://www.stuaff.niu.edu/uhs/norms.htm); University of Arizona, (http://www.health. arizona. edu); Western Washington University, (http://www.ac.wwu.edu/~chw/prev_well.html).

Diversity

Examples of effective programs aimed at diversity issues are presented here.

CommUNITY Education Program. The CommUNITY Education Program is designed to educate residence hall students about issues of diversity, and to create leaders in the residence halls outside of the resident assistant function. These student leaders are known as Community Educators (CUEs) and they live throughout the various residence halls. The role of the CUEs is to design programs around various topics related to diversity, to lead others in discussions of sensitive topics and in exploration of identity and self-perception, and to model appropriate behavior, attitudes, values, and beliefs without denying each student's uniqueness. The goals of the program include building community within the residence halls, challenging assumptions, creating dialogue, and fostering acceptance among all students. Contact: Barry Magee, Assistant to the Director for Student Programs and Services, Indiana University. E-mail: (cue@indiana.edu).

A Different Life: Growing Up Gay. The purpose of the Growing Up Gay program is to facilitate exploration of the issues and obstacles that gay, lesbian, bisexual, and transgender students face. The facilitator first asks participants to fill out six index cards with specific information, such as their favorite place or the name of a person very close to them. The facilitator then reads a story about what it might be like to grow up gay; during the reading, the participants must rip up their cards as they lose the things written on them when they "come out." After the exercise, participants discuss how they felt ripping up the cards, how their experiences growing up were both different and similar to those in the story, and how they can work to change the reality presented in the story. The text of the story can be found on-line at (http://www.residentassistant.com). Contact Dan Oltersdorf, Colorado State University. E-mail: (dano@peakpeak.com). Web site: (http://www.residentassistant.com).

Campus Diversity Leadership Team. The National Coalition Building Institute (NCBI) currently has diversity leadership teams on over forty-five college campuses across the United States. The program offers a systematic approach to welcoming diversity as well as an ongoing mechanism for staff, faculty, and students to provide an institutional response to racism. These goals are accomplished by recruiting and training a cadre of student leaders, administrators, and faculty who act as a leadership team that is fully empowered to confront tough campus issues.

A NCBI campus team begins with a three-day Train-the-Trainers seminar. In this session, participants learn how to lead the NCBI prejudice reduction workshop. This workshop is a one-day event that can also be incorporated into classroom curricula. The workshop includes a set of activities that helps participants celebrate their similarities and differences, identify the misinformation that they have learned about other groups, identify and heal from internalized oppression, and claim pride in their own group identities. Participants also learn about the personal impact of discrimination through the telling of individual stories and become empowered by learning concrete tools for changing bigoted comments and actions. Participants learn to lead the NCBI Controversial Issue Process as well. This process helps individuals and groups to reframe heated emotional or political debates by learning to take the heartfelt concerns of each side into account.

The leadership team meets once a month on campus to receive ongoing training and support, plan training sessions, and design ways to serve as a campus resource. The campus team has intervened during student and faculty protests, and has served as a resource in situations involving conflict based on race, gender, or sexual orientation in university departments. Contact: Kevin Shollenberger, National Director for NCBI Campus Programs, Columbia University, Lerner Hall—Room 403, 2920 Broadway–mc2601, New York N.Y. 10027. E-mail: (HYPERLINK mailto:ks693@Columbia.edu (ks693@Columbia.edu),

Voices From the Community: Memphians Celebrate Diversity. Voices From the Community: Memphians Celebrate Diversity was a day-long festival of music, poetry readings, storytelling, story circles, art talks, and an art exhibition, all by diverse local artists and practitioners. Students from area colleges and universities representing a wide variety of cultural backgrounds formed a panel to discuss issues of identity and ethnicity from a student viewpoint. The centerpiece of the day was the production of "Messages of Peace," placed at the heart of the program, to provide participants with various means to express their ideas on diversity. An eighteen-foot canvas, divided into seventy-seven panels, gave artists the opportunity to paint images representing their ideas about race and diversity; an inscription book was provided for written statements. Local media personalities interviewed attendees on their ideas about community and diversity. All of these messages will form a permanent record of Memphian voices and backdrops for future community events. Contact: Barbara S. Frankle, Associate Dean for Academic Affairs, 807 Walker Avenue, LeMoyne-Owen College, Memphis, Tenn. 38126. Telephone: (901) 942-7363. E-mail: (barbara_frankle@nile.lemoyne-owen.edu).

Color Me Human. To increase the number of opportunities to promote diversity on campus, the Student Life Department at Hawkeye Community College created the Color Me Human program. A comprehensive plan to increase awareness of diversity on campus, as well as build individual commitment and community among students, faculty, and staff, the program places a high priority on training student leaders to become influential voices that value diversity and create innovative ways to engage participants on campus in dialogue on issues such as gender, age, and race relations. The Student Life Department considers the program a process that moves individuals and small groups through a progressive continuum that includes tolerance, acceptance, respect, and the celebration of diversity. Program participants design cocurricular activities to address these various levels of the continuum and to increase self-awareness, foster community, and develop leadership skills among the attendees. Past activities included a forum featuring the perspectives of students with disabilities, an international food festival, and a presentation at Martin Luther King, Jr. Day. Those who attend these events receive a Color Me Human button that symbolizes self-awareness and sensitivity for diversity and reminds wearers of the importance of celebrating diversity on campus every day. Contact: Ruben Carrion, Director of Student Life, 1501 East Orange Road, P.O. Box 8015, Hawkeye Community College, Waterloo, Iowa 50702. Telephone: (319) 296-4027. E-mail: (rcarrion@hawkeye.cc.ia.us).

International Festival. Each spring, the Community College of Philadelphia holds an International Festival featuring students sharing music, food, dance, poetry, and other representations of their cultural heritage. The week-long festival also features international films, guest speakers, and visiting performers. Each year, the organizers select a theme that will potentially weave a unifying strand across differences. The organizers also sponsor poetry and essay contests as well as provide visual displays to express the chosen theme; a recent theme was "It Takes Village to Raise a Child." The week began with a lecture on the musical instruments of Indochina, Asia, and East Africa, and continued with performances of Cherokee dances and Haitian, Vietnamese, and Filipino songs and dances. Also included were demonstrations of the Japanese tea ceremony, Caribbean mask-making, urban jump rope games, and Tai Chi. An international storytelling program for children concluded the week. Contact: David Prejsnar, Coordinator of International Education, Community College of Philadelphia, 1700 Spring Garden Street, Philadelphia, Pa. 19130-3991. E-mail: (dprejsnar@ccp.cc.pa.us)

World Wide Web Resources for Programming

1. National Service-Learning Clearinghouse http://www.nicsl.coled.umn.edu
   The Learn and Serve American National Service-Learning Clearinghouse is a comprehensive information system that focuses on all

dimensions of service learning covering kindergarten through higher education, school-based as well as community-based initiatives.

2. Campus Outreach Opportunity League http://www.cool2serve.org
   The Campus Outreach Opportunity League is a national, nonprofit organization dedicated to the education and empowerment of college students to strengthen the nation through community service.

3. Lambda 10 Project: National Clearinghouse for Gay, Lesbian, and Bisexual Greek Issues http://www.indiana.edu/~lambda10
   The Lambda 10 Project works to heighten the visibility of gay, lesbian, and bisexual members of the college fraternity and sorority communities by serving as a clearinghouse for educational resources and educational materials related to sexual orientation and the fraternity/sorority experience.

4. DiversityWeb http://www.inform.umd.edu/DiversityWeb/
   DiversityWeb is part of a larger communications initiative entitled DiversityWorks, which is designed to create new pathways for diversity collaboration and connection, via the World Wide Web and more traditional forms of print communication.

5. Student Activities Offices Online http://dolphin.upenn.edu/~oslaf/saos.html
   This page provides an alphabetical listing of links to the Web sites of student activities offices at colleges and universities across the United States.

6. American College Personnel Association Commission III: Housing and Residential Life Model Programs
   This site provides descriptions and contact information for programs chosen as model programs by Commission III.

7. American College Personnel Association Commission IV: Students, Their Activities, and Their Community http://www.acpa.nche.edu/comms/comm04
   The focus of this commission is on the college student and his or her environment, specifically the student's involvement in the out-of-classroom learning environment and the larger community. This site includes links to the Commission IV newsletter that cites model programs.

8. BACCHUS and GAMMA Peer Education Network http://www.bacchusgamma.org
   The BACCHUS and GAMMA Peer Education Network is an international association of college- and university-based peer education programs focusing on alcohol abuse prevention and other related student health and safety issues. Programming manuals for Sexual Responsibility Week, National Collegiate Alcohol Awareness Week, and Safe Spring Break programs can be downloaded from the site.

9. ResidentAssistant.com http://www.residentassistant.com
   A resource for resident assistants to augment the resources and training provided by their residence life staff, this site includes programming ideas, advice from other resident assistants, and discussion groups.

10. RESNet http://www.housing.ucf.edu/RESNet
    RESNet allows residence life staff members to share ideas for program-
    ming, newsletter fillers, and motivational tidbits.
11. Association of College Unions International http://www.indiana.
    edu/~acui
    The mission of the association is to advance the role of the college
    union as well as to help members improve their programs and services
    and be effective contributors to individual growth and development.
    The site contains links to educational information and resources for
    campus programming.

References

Berkowitz, A. D. "In Practice—The Proactive Prevention Model: Helping Students Trans-
late Healthy Beliefs into Healthy Actions." *About Campus,* 1998, 4(3) 26–27.
Haines, M. "A Social Norms Approach to Preventing Binge Drinking at Colleges and Universities." Newton, Mass.: Higher Education Center for Alcohol and Other Drug Prevention, 1998. (EDD00001)
Perkins, H.W. "College Student Misperceptions of Alcohol and Other Drug Norms
Among Peers: Exploring Cause, Consequences, and Implications for Prevention Programs" In *Designing Alcohol and Other Drug Prevention Programs in Higher Education:
Bringing Theory into Practice.* Newton, Mass.: Higher Education Center for Alcohol
and Other Drug Prevention, 1997.

*HEATHER O'NEILL is a second-year master's student in the Student Development
in Postsecondary Education Program at The University of Iowa, Iowa City.*

INDEX

Back Issue/Subscription Order Form

Copy or detach and send to:
Jossey-Bass Inc., Publishers, 350 Sansome Street, San Francisco, CA 94104-1342

Call or fax toll free!
Phone 888-378-2537 6AM-5PM PST; Fax 800-605-2665

Back issues: Please send me the following issues at $23 each
(Important: please include series initials and issue number, such as SS90)

1. SS _____

_____

_____

$ _____ Total for single issues

$ _____ Shipping charges (for single issues *only;* subscriptions are exempt
from shipping charges): Up to $30, add $5^{50} • $30^{01}–$50, add $6^{50}
$50^{01}–$75, add $8 • $75^{01}–$100, add $10 • $100^{01}–$150, add $12
Over $150, call for shipping charge

Subscriptions   Please ❏ start ❏ renew my subscription to *New Directions
for Student Services* for the year _____ at the following rate:

U.S.:   ❏ Individual $58   ❏ Institutional $104

Canada: ❏ Individual $83   ❏ Institutional $129

All others: ❏ Individual $88   ❏ Institutional $134

NOTE: Subscriptions are quarterly, and are for the calendar year only.
Subscriptions begin with the spring issue of the year indicated above.

$ _____ Total single issues and subscriptions (Add appropriate sales tax for
your state for single issue orders. No sales tax for U.S. subscriptions. NY
and Canadian residents, add GST for subscriptions and single issues.)

❏ Payment enclosed (U.S. check or money order only)

❏ VISA, MC, AmEx, Discover Card #_____ Exp. date_____

Signature _____ Day phone _____

❏ Bill me (U.S. institutional orders only. Purchase order required)

Purchase order #_____

Federal Tax ID 135593032 GST 89102-8052

Name _____

Address _____

_____

Phone_____ E-mail _____

For more information about Jossey-Bass Publishers, visit our Web site at:
www.josseybass.com   **PRIORITY CODE = ND1**

OTHER TITLES AVAILABLE IN THE
NEW DIRECTIONS FOR STUDENT SERVICES SERIES
John H. Schuh, Editor-in-Chief
Elizabeth J. Whitt, Associate Editor